GUIDE

CW00917067

May–August 2018

Edited by **David Spriggs**

The Bible Reading Fellowship
15 The Chambers, Vineyard
Abingdon OX14 3FE
brf.org.uk

The Bible Reading Fellowship (BRF) is a Registered Charity (233280)

ISBN 978 0 85746 603 7

Distributed in Australia by:
MediaCom Education Inc, PO Box 610, Unley, SA 5061
Tel: 1 800 811 311 | admin@mediacom.org.au

Distributed in New Zealand by:
Scripture Union Wholesale, PO Box 760, Wellington
Tel: 04 385 0421 | suwholesale@clear.net.nz

Acknowledgements
Scripture quotations taken from the New American Standard Bible®, Copyright © 1960, 1962, 1963, 1968, 1971, 1972, 1973, 1975, 1977, 1995 by The Lockman Foundation. Used by permission. (www.Lockman.org)

Scripture quotations taken from The Holy Bible, New International Version (Anglicised edition) copyright © 1979, 1984, 2011 by Biblica. Used by permission of Hodder & Stoughton Publishers, a Hachette UK company. All rights reserved. 'NIV' is a registered trademark of Biblica. UK trademark number 1448790.

Scripture quotations from The New Revised Standard Version of the Bible, Anglicised edition, copyright © 1989, 1995 by the Division of Christian Education of the National Council of the Churches of Christ in the United States of America. Used by permission. All rights reserved.

Scripture quotations taken from the Holy Bible, English Standard Version, published by HarperCollins Publishers, © 2001 Crossway Bibles, a division of Good News Publishers. Used by permission. All rights reserved.

Scripture quotations taken from the New English Bible, copyright © Cambridge University Press and Oxford University Press 1961, 1970. All rights reserved.

Scripture quotations taken from the Jerusalem Bible © 1966, 1967, 1968 by Darton, Longman & Todd Ltd and Doubleday & Company, Inc.

Printed by Gutenberg Press, Tarxien, Malta

Suggestions for using *Guidelines*

Set aside a regular time and place, if possible, when you can read and pray undisturbed. Before you begin, take time to be still and, if you find it helpful, use the BRF Prayer on page 6.

In *Guidelines*, the introductory section provides context for the passages or themes to be studied, while the units of comment can be used daily, weekly, or whatever best fits your timetable. You will need a Bible (more than one if you want to compare different translations) as Bible passages are not included. At the end of each week is a 'Guidelines' section, offering further thoughts about or practical application of what you have been studying.

Occasionally, you may read something in *Guidelines* that you find particularly challenging, even uncomfortable. This is inevitable in a series of notes which draws on a wide spectrum of contributors, and doesn't believe in ducking difficult issues. Indeed, we believe that *Guidelines* readers much prefer thought-provoking material to a bland diet that only confirms what they already think.

If you do disagree with a contributor, you may find it helpful to go through these three steps. First, think about why you feel uncomfortable. Perhaps this is an idea that is new to you, or you are not happy at the way something has been expressed. Or there may be something more substantial – you may feel that the writer is guilty of sweeping generalisation, factual error, theological or ethical misjudgement. Second, pray that God would use this disagreement to teach you more about his word and about yourself. Third, think about what you will do as a result of the disagreement. You might resolve to find out more about the issue, or write to the contributor or the editors of *Guidelines*.

To send feedback, please email **enquiries@brf.org.uk**, phone **+44 (0)1865 319700** or write to the address shown opposite.

Writers in this issue

Jeremy Duff is Principal of St Padarn's Institute, a new centre for ministry training in Wales. His book *The Elements of New Testament Greek* (2005) is Cambridge University Press's bestselling religion title. He has also written *Peter's Preaching* for BRF (2015).

Brian Howell is visiting lecturer in Old Testament at London School of Theology. Previously he served as the Dean of Studies for Bible Society. He has published on interpreting divine metaphors, and currently researches the *Imago Dei* when not playing saxophone.

Graham Dow retired in 2009 after being Bishop of Carlisle for eight years, Bishop of Willesden (London) and Vicar of Holy Trinity Church, Coventry for eleven years. He loves expounding the Bible, supporting Holy Spirit renewal, praying for healing, the liberation of lay ministry and God's purpose in daily work.

Steve Motyer loves the quest for understanding – and the Bible is central to this quest. His life as a carer helps with this, as does 30 years of teaching New Testament and Counselling at London School of Theology.

Ian Paul is Associate Minister at St Nic's Nottingham, and Honorary Assistant Professor at the University of Nottingham, as well as Managing Editor at Grove Books in Cambridge. He blogs at **www.psephizo.com**.

Henry Wansbrough OSB is a monk at Ampleforth Abbey in Yorkshire. He is a member of the Anglican Roman Catholic International Commission, and lectures frequently across the globe. He has recently completed a new translation of the Bible, the *Revised New Jerusalem Bible*.

Ian Macnair worked in church pastoral ministry, Bible College lecturing and administration before his retirement. His writings include *Teach Yourself New Testament Greek* (Nelson, 1995).

David Spriggs writes...

At the heart of this issue we are celebrating the life-giving festival of Pentecost. Jeremy Duff, on the Spirit in Acts, explores with us how the unfolding story of the life of the early church is in reality the story of the Holy Spirit guiding, empowering and blessing the obedience of those first Christians. It is a remarkable account and holds many clues and prompts for us as Christians today as we seek to live faithfully in a complex and ever-changing culture.

But at the heart of our witness for Christ is the character which the Holy Spirit produces within. Ian Macnair brings his biblical scholarship and pastoral experience to the well-known list of characteristics we call the fruit of the Spirit. He makes two fundamental points: first that this 'menu' is not a pick-and-mix one – we are called to allow God to grow them all in us; and secondly that while God's Spirit produces them, we still need to pursue them!

Steve Motyer provides us with the narrative picture of Jesus to enrich our understanding of who we are called to be as he continues his journey in Mark's Gospel. We can glimpse a great deal about the heart of Jesus as we see him conquering the storm, demonic forces and biting criticism – all situations which require the fruit of the Spirit to handle as Jesus did.

Bishop Graham Dow shows us how the Bible can help us understand and respond to the demonic forces around us and how we can contribute to God's mission in this context as he explores 'deliverance'.

Ian Paul's exposition of 2 Timothy, Titus and Philemon, amongst other things, shows how the fruit of the Spirit was no abstract moral list but was exemplified in the life of Paul and needed in the ongoing life of the churches.

Brian Howell's insights on the book of Genesis remind us that the development of the early church and its mission has an antecedent in the way God starts to form his people, the nation of Israel as his 'mission partner' to bring to fruition his purposes to redeem his broken creation. Hence we are constantly reminded of the larger cultural context and the global vision of God.

Two other Old Testament contributions are Leviticus in the capable hands of Henry Wansbrough, and the prophets Zephaniah and Habakkuk, which are intriguing if less well-known. Zephaniah seems to be a catalogue of the judgement of God on Israel and the nations, yet it also contains the amazing promise that he will remedy their rebellion, take away the judgement against them and renew them in his love. Habakkuk brings his own challenges to us: 'He shows us a way to grow in our faith by boldly putting the tough questions of life back to the God who raised them.'

May God equip us for every good work as we respond to his word.

The BRF Prayer

Almighty God,
you have taught us that your word is a lamp for our feet
and a light for our path. Help us, and all who prayerfully
read your word, to deepen our fellowship with you
and with each other through your love.
And in so doing may we come to know you more fully,
love you more truly, and follow more faithfully
in the steps of your son Jesus Christ, who lives and reigns
with you and the Holy Spirit, one God for evermore.
Amen

The Spirit in Acts

Jeremy Duff

The Acts of the Apostles is the linchpin of the New Testament. It holds together the Gospels and the letters. Furthermore, it portrays the apostles as united – that the different figures in early Christianity were part of the same movement, with different emphases perhaps, but finding agreement, and that they were in step with Jesus. Thus we approach the New Testament as a single entity – looking to the letters to illuminate the Jesus of the Gospels, and assuming that the different letters from James, Paul, Peter and John can be brought into harmony.

Acts speaks particularly about mission and evangelism, and the Spirit. Of all the books in the New Testament it is Acts, since it deals with the 'life and work of the Church', which sets out most clearly the way in which God continues to act in the lives of Jesus' disciples – through the Spirit. Hence our topic for these next two weeks – the Spirit in Acts. In these notes, we will cover every reference to the Spirit in the book of Acts, as a guard against us just picking our favourite passages or those which confirm our views!

The book of Acts was written as the 'second half' of the Gospel of Luke (see Luke 1:1–4; Acts 1:1–2). It is reasonable to assume that its author was a 'Luke', if only because it is not the name of an apostle. Scholars are suspicious of texts bearing the name of important figures in as much as you could understand why a 'powerful name' might be added to a text, but if the author wasn't called Luke it's hard to know where this name would have come from. The presence of five sections in Acts where the author uses 'we' (16:10–17; most of 20; 21:1–18; much of 27 and 28) would naturally imply that the author travelled with Paul. Colossians 4:14, 2 Timothy 4:11 and Philemon 1:24 develop this to reach the conclusion, also accepted by the early church, that Luke and Acts were written by one of Paul's companions, called Luke.

It is conventional to use the pronouns 'he', 'him', and 'his' when referring to the Spirit. This is not because of any claim or assumption that the Spirit is any more 'male' than 'female'; but to avoid the use of 'it' which seems to downgrade the Spirit from a 'person' (who can choose things) to a force.

I stick to this convention throughout these notes.

Quotations are expressed in my own translation; the notes can be used with any modern English Bible.

1 Jesus continues his work

Acts 1:1–9

This is not the beginning. This is not just an interesting fact – it matters because of the words 'began to' in verse 1. In the former book, the Gospel of Luke, Jesus 'began to' do and teach, which raises the expectation that he will continue to do so in this second volume. But surely Jesus ascends in verse 9 and is no longer a key actor in the story (excepting perhaps his appearance to Paul in Acts 9)?

Presumably the point is that Jesus continues to act throughout all we are going to read, either through the apostles, or indeed through the Holy Spirit. We will see the apostles acting as Jesus did (e.g. bringing healing, 3:1–10; or willingly facing death, 21:10–15) and Paul would describe the believers as 'the body of Christ', though this language isn't used within Acts (though persecuting the church is seen as persecuting Jesus, 9:5). The Spirit is presented as a 'replacement Jesus' – one must go for the other to come (vv. 4–9; 3:19–21; though the language is never as developed as in John's Gospel, e.g. John 14:15–26). As we read on, we will realise that it is God who is in control; indeed, some claim the book should be titled 'the acts of the Holy Spirit', not of the apostles. Perhaps it is foolish to try to separate these two options. After all, it is the Spirit who enables the apostles (v. 8; 4:8; 6:10; compare Luke 12:11–12). In the words of Acts 5:32, 'We are witnesses of these things, and so is the Holy Spirit.' Either way, Jesus is not stuck in history – he is at work.

Baptism in the Spirit is a phrase we hear on John the Baptist's lips (Luke 3:16–17), where it seems to be connected to judgement, or at least 'refining'. This connects with Joel 2:28–31, quoted in Acts 2:16–21, where the pouring out of the Spirit 'in the last days' is linked to the 'day of the Lord'. This is how the apostles understand it – hence they respond to Jesus' mention of baptism in the Spirit with a question about restoring the kingdom to Israel

(v. 6). Jesus' reply, though, gives a different twist. This receipt of the Spirit brings in a period of witnessing, and gives power for that task (v. 8). Our minds are to be turned away from thinking of 'the end', or other theological speculation, and instead focused on a task. After all, Jesus has only begun his work and yet he is now 'offstage' (v. 9) – together the apostles and the Spirit need to act.

2 The Spirit comes

Acts 2:1–16

This is the moment. The waiting (1:4) is over. The Spirit is poured out and received. The image of 'tongues of fire' has a dual function. It connects back John the Baptist's language of baptism with the Spirit and fire (Luke 3:17) but also connects forward to the idea of speaking in different tongues ('tongues' is the same word as 'languages').

It is certainly a moment of 'power' – not just the powerful wind but the powerful effect it has on those there ('astonished', v. 7; 'astonished and perplexed', v. 12) which provokes response (vv. 12–13).

Some see the miracle of the languages as a 'reverse' of the tower of Babel story – a symbolic 'reversal' of division we find in our fallen world (Genesis 11:1–9). There are intriguing echoes in the details: they were building a city with its top in heaven (where Jesus has now departed to – Acts 1:9; 3:21; 7:55); they were going to make a name for themselves (the name of Jesus is constant in Acts e.g. 2:21, 38; 3:6, 16) and nothing would be impossible for them.

More immediately, we should connect this passage to Acts 1:8 – you will receive power when the Spirit comes, and be witnesses to the ends of the earth. The 'ends of the earth' have come (v. 5) and the Spirit gives the apostles the power, the ability, to witness to them by enabling them to speak in other languages (v. 4). It would be foolish to see this event as 'completing' Jesus' command – the world is a far bigger place than can fit into a public space in Jerusalem – it is an event which points to a bigger reality. Perhaps the same can be said of the different languages. The Spirit giving the ability to witness despite the most obvious barrier of language is a pointer to a bigger reality that the Spirit gives the ability to witness across all barriers, of fear, culture, background and history.

Notice that the powerful miracle itself doesn't 'witness' well. It communicates that *something* is happening, but *what* is unclear. It can be interpreted as bad (drunk, v. 13) as well as good. This points to a deeper truth. Often we imagine that 'power from on high' would bring people to God – 'if I see a miracle I would believe'. It's a convenient belief because it shifts responsibility away from us. Here, though, we see that the eye-catching event (the miracle, the life turned around, the setting up of the food bank) might provoke a question, but witnesses are needed to give it meaning.

3 The Spirit for everyone

Acts 2:17–39

This passage is so rich that we have to focus our attention on the references to the Spirit – two near the beginning (vv. 17–18) and two near the end (vv. 33, 38).

Peter starts by answering the question. The people have heard the surprising speech of Jesus' followers, and so Peter refers them to Joel 2:28–32. The word order in the Greek makes the point clearly: 'I will pour out my spirit on all flesh and they will prophesy… I will pour out my spirit and they will prophesy' (vv. 17–18). The Spirit's action is to make people speak out, just as they are doing that day. Consider also Ezekiel 2:1–7, where the Spirit enters Ezekiel because he has a commission to speak to the rebellious people of Israel and needs not to be afraid of them.

Peter answers the question provoked by the event, but doesn't leave it there. He goes on to tell the story he wants to tell, the story of Jesus and how it affects them. The Spirit gives the insight and boldness to identify how God is at work and to speak out 'what is really going on', which is a good description of prophecy.

As he nears the end of his speech, he brings it back to what the people have seen (v. 33: 'what you now see and hear'). The Spirit is called the 'promised Holy Spirit' (v. 33), which reminds us of Jesus' promise to send the Spirit on the apostles (1:4–5, 9) but also of parts of the Old Testament such as Joel. What has happened is amazing, but is in keeping with what we know of God already. God does do new things, yet they are in continuity with his revelation in the past.

The description of the 'chain' in the reception of the Spirit – Father to Jesus to them – is important. It emphasises the centrality of Jesus. He is not a stage in God's plan that is now history. Jesus is the one continuing to act. It also suggests that Jesus is 'God for us' – it is through relating to him that we receive God's gifts (v. 38). The Spirit is the confirmation that God is at work in the apostles, and it is the gift which allows others to join them, for it is available to all – young and old, male and female, the weak, children and those far off (vv. 17–18, 39) – through Jesus.

4 The Spirit of boldness

Acts 4:1–12, 23–31

This passage continues on from Acts 2 about the role of the Spirit and develops it further. We have the same sequence. The activity of Jesus' disciples creates disturbance (v. 2; v. 9 points back to the disturbance caused by the healing in ch. 3). This produces a mixed reaction – growth and opposition (vv. 3–4) – just as the reception of the Spirit at Pentecost produced amazement and the accusation of drunkenness. The negative response, however, is itself highly productive – it gives opportunity for explanation (vv. 7–11).

Peter's speech has many similarities with his speech at Pentecost – he starts with the 'disturbance' which has raised the question, moves on to 'tell the story' of Jesus, and concludes with a focus on the salvation available through 'the name' (vv. 8–12). Here, Peter is explicitly said to be 'full of the Holy Spirit', in such as a way as to suggest that this is the reason he spoke as he did.

What difference did the Spirit make to Peter's speech? Twice in Luke's Gospel Jesus has spoken about situations like these – Luke 12:11–12 and 21:12–15. There he tells the disciples not to worry about how to defend themselves; they will be given what to say. If you look at the detail, there is an interesting variation. In Luke 12, the Spirit will give them what to say; in Luke 21, Jesus will, and by the end of our passage it is '*they*' who are speaking 'the word of God' (v. 31). Jesus' work is carried out by the Spirit (Acts 1:1) and now by his Spirit-filled disciples. The Spirit means they need not worry and, furthermore, makes them bold (v. 31: 'filled with the Spirit… spoke the word of God *boldly*'). This is further emphasised by the context. A few months earlier, Jesus had been brought before a similar group of religious leaders. Within 24 hours, he was dead. Peter should have been terrified.

Peter is well aware of this precedent – he refers to it in his speech (v. 11). But he now sees these events in a different light. They fulfil the word spoken by the Spirit in Psalm 2:1–2 (vv. 25–26) – that is, this situation conforms to the pattern outlined there. These authorities 'raged' and 'plotted' against Jesus, but it was all 'in vain' – for God raised him from the dead, reversing their sentence. So too now their actions against Peter will be 'in vain'. The Spirit gives the courage necessary for Peter to be a witness. Our passage ends with the disciples praying that they may be enabled to witness with boldness. How is this answered? By them receiving the Spirit (vv. 29–31). Jesus told the disciples that receiving the Spirit would give them the power to be witnesses (Acts 1:8). It seems that a major element of that power is courage. Do we recognise this as our major need?

5 God's presence

Acts 5:1–11

The death penalty for not giving enough to church? Church treasurers might cheer, but many of us might think this a little excessive! Execution for fraud is not a lot better. What is going on here?

The clue comes at the end of verse 4: 'You didn't lie to humans but to God'. How did Sapphira and Ananias lie to God? It's an odd concept when you think about it. I might hide from God, and sometimes I might be self-deluded, and I might lie to other people, but lying to God is more unusual because we tend to be aware that God knows the truth.

What they did was act falsely and speak false words to the Christian community. What this passage seems to illustrate is that this was effectively the same as lying to God (compare Acts 9:1–4, where persecuting the Christian community is described as persecuting Jesus). The Spirit was present in the community to such an extent that lying to it was lying to the Spirit (vv. 3, 9). Indeed one might now say that the Spirit dwells in the community of disciples in the way that people might have thought of God's Spirit dwelling in the temple. Elements of Jesus' teaching seemed to emerge from the idea that God's presence was now to be found in him not in the temple (e.g. John 1:14; 2:20–22; Mark 1:40—2:12, since the temple was the place where cleansing and forgiveness were received). Ephesians 2:21 and 1 Peter 2:5 speak of the Christian community as a temple. This is made more explicit in 2 Corinthians 6:16: 'We are the temple of the living God,' and 1 Corinthians 6:19: 'Your body is a temple of the Holy Spirit.' Closest to our passage, however, is 1 Corinthians 3:16–17: 'Do you not know that you are God's temple and that God's Spirit lives in you? If anyone destroys God's temple, God will destroy them. For God's temple is holy, and that is you.' (Note the 'you' here is plural – the Christian community.)

It would be a mistake to jump from this passage to any idea which suggests that God is contained within the church, or that the church as an institution wields God's power, or should be treated like God. Indeed, we might still struggle with the idea of people dying for attacking God's temple, though in the cultural context of Acts, death as the outcome for desecrating a temple would not have been so shocking. What we take away is the underlying point. Through the Spirit, God was present in this community of disciples of Jesus to such an extent that it was like the most holy place in the temple. The Spirit is not just 'in each of us' but is, or at least could be, in 'us as a community of disciples' in more powerful ways than we might imagine.

6 Spirit-empowered service

Acts 6:1–15

The Spirit equipped Stephen, and the other six, for the task of distributing food. Is that surprising? I hope not. Practical ministry is just as much ministry, and as needful of God's Spirit, as 'preaching' or other ministries more associated with clergy or 'the minister'. Sadly, we tend not to believe that or communicate it and instead divide 'ministries' into the more practical ones which are just a matter of willingness, or having the skills and other more 'spiritual' ones to which you need to be 'called'. Indeed, most of our Bible translations twist this passage in that way because they translate the Greek work *diakonia* differently: in verse 1 ('distribution' of food) and verse 4 ('ministry' of the word). Acts actually says that handling the food and handling the word are both 'ministry' (*diakonia*) and for both the Spirit is needed. It might be better if we translated the word as 'service' throughout.

Perhaps underlying this is our difficulty to believe that God is interested in our bodies as well as our 'souls'. Or those teaching us the Bible have (inadvertently, I am sure) implied that their sort of 'service' is more 'spiritual' than the 'service' offered by others. This hasn't been helped by the practice in some denominations of linking this passage to 'deacons' who are a form of clergy, who in fact preach and within a year or two become priests often leading churches. So, this passage which highlights the Spirit empowering people for practical service is taken over by clergy as applying to them.

Verses 8 to 15 reveal that one of the seven then became a miracle worker and speaker, described in a similar way to the apostles. We see the same pattern as with Peter. What Stephen did created opportunity for him to speak, which he took even though he didn't have the words, because it is the Spirit which speaks through him (v. 10). Indeed he ends up being accused in a similar manner to how Jesus was, and in the face of this attack his face is like an angel (v. 15), presumably a sign that God was with him, through his Spirit.

We miss the point if we think Stephen was a good speaker. He was chosen to do practical duties – to wait on tables. But the Spirit was at work in him so his actions provoked opportunity to speak, and the Spirit then gave him amazing words to say. The Spirit transforms normal people into powerful witnesses.

Guidelines

Where is the Spirit found? What does he do? Our readings this week have circled round these questions. The answers need to be pondered.

We have seen that the Spirit is found in everyone who has turned to Jesus – in the young and old, the waiters and the fishermen – and he is to be found in some important sense in the community of disciples as a whole. How do we make space for the Spirit to be working through 'the unlikely'? Indeed, maybe that is you, and you think that because all you do is work in a café, like Stephen, the Spirit can't really use you. How do we make sense of the Spirit being present within the community of disciples as a whole? That we are not just a collection of individuals but together we are a place, a body, which God inhabits? A first step might be to consider, with Ananias and Sapphira in mind, whether our community life, the values we live out, our way of acting as a church, is appropriate for the place where God is present.

What does the Spirit do? Interestingly, the dominant answer we have seen in these chapters is that he makes us bold to witness; he gives us the courage we need to testify to Jesus, and the words which explain what people see. This is partly giving the words to say. But the main thing seems to be giving the courage to speak. Can you recognise this? We may tell ourselves we don't speak because we don't have the words, but really what is lacking is courage. Dare we ask the Spirit to give us more courage?

1 Resisting the Spirit

Acts 7:1–3, 48–60

'You always resist the Holy Spirit' (v. 51). These are condemning words. They take us back to the story of Ananias and Sapphira, where defrauding the community is tantamount to 'lying to the Spirit' – a sacrilege deserving the same punishment as desecrating the temple. Indeed the context here is very similar. For while Stephen's main point is that the people have always resisted God, a key part of the accusation against him was about the temple (Acts 6:13–14) and Stephen finishes on this point (vv. 48–50). 'Where is God to be found?' – he is present in people like Stephen.

We might also look back to Jesus' words in Luke 12:10: 'And everyone who speaks a word against the Son of Man will be forgiven, but anyone who blasphemes against the Holy Spirit will not be forgiven.' 'Blaspheming against the Holy Spirit' seems in the Gospels (e.g. Mark 3:22–30) to mean not being able to recognise God's activity or labelling it as the devil's work (hence the lack of forgiveness because if you can't recognise God, how can you turn to him?). That is what the leaders are accused of in verse 52. Certainly not recognising, not even just resisting, but actually killing God's 'Righteous One'.

Stephen's retelling of the Old Testament story also makes a further powerful claim. For Stephen is putting Jesus in the line of the prophets, and continues that line to people like him (see Luke 11:51–52). The Spirit who is at work in Stephen (v. 55) is the same as who worked throughout the Old Testament (v. 53; compare Acts 1:16 and 28:25 where it is explicitly about people resisting God). This paints the authorities into the role of the disobedient or rebellious part of God's people, those who 'harden their hearts' (Psalm 95:8). In effect, Stephen claims that they, the Sanhedrin, are now a backwater; the story of God's faithful people is carrying on through people like him.

Verses 59 and 60 closely echo Jesus' death. Stephen is following in the pattern of Jesus (as later Paul will; see Acts 20:22; 21:11–14). His vision of the Son of Man (vv. 55–56) echoes Jesus' word at his trial: 'From now, the Son of Man will be seated at the right hand of the mighty God' (Luke 22:69). But the last chapter of Luke and these first seven of Acts have demonstrated that God was with Jesus. The Sanhedrin which condemned Jesus continues its resistance to God's Spirit by condemning Stephen. God's story, marked out by the presence of the Spirit, is passing them by.

2 Who receives the Spirit?

Acts 8:9–25

What meaning do we draw from the fact that the Samaritans didn't receive the Spirit at baptism, but only when Peter and John laid their hands on them (vv. 15–17)? First, we note that the Simon story is probably interwoven with this story about the reception of the Spirit in Samaria because it illustrates a point. What point? Well, Simon voices the idea that the apostles have the power or ability to give the Holy Spirit to others (vv. 18–19). Clearly he is wrong to offer to pay, but he is also wrong in thinking that the apostles can 'give out' the Spirit. When you read the text carefully you see that, aside from 'laying on of hands', the apostles pray that the Samaritans might receive the Spirit (from God) (vv. 15–17). The Spirit comes *from God*; 'passing on the Spirit' is not an ability any human can have.

So why did the believers not receive the Spirit until Peter and John prayed? Across Christian history, this passage has been used to support distortions which suggest that trusting in Jesus, or being baptised, are not sufficient – a 'second stage' is needed, perhaps a visible experience of the Holy Spirit (e.g. speaking in tongues) or a particular church rite (e.g. confirmation by a bishop). While this passage might encourage such a view, it is out of step with the rest of scripture (e.g. Romans 8:9–11; 10:9–10; Galatians 4:6).

The best approach is to connect this to the 'breaking the boundaries' which mission to the Samaritans represented, for they were 'half-Jews' at best, while up to this point in Acts only Jews had believed. Indeed, the presence of Simon the magician there only confirms this impression that Samaritans were not 'proper' Jews. Our passage highlights the fact that the Samaritans received the Spirit, while also reminding us that the Spirit only comes because God sends him – it is God, not people, who is deciding to bless them in this way. Thus, there can be no doubt that God indeed did welcome these 'half-Jews'. We will see the same again when the first Gentile comes to faith – Cornelius in Acts 10.

The Peter and John link is still intriguing. We get something similar when Paul has to pray for 'disciples' he meets in Ephesus to receive the Spirit (Acts

19:1–7). My view is that it reinforces the sense that the disciples form 'one family' and that coming to faith in Jesus involves not just belief and trust in him, but joining the existing family of believers. The Samaritans received the Spirit as they joined the disciples in Jerusalem through the encounter with Jerusalem's representatives Peter and John. (Later in Acts 9:31, Samaria is mentioned in the same breath as Judea and Galilee as part of the growing church – singular, a single family – encouraged by the Spirit.)

3 Breaking boundaries

Acts 11:1–18

We have jumped three sections of Acts in which the Spirit is mentioned. First, Philip is clearly led by the Spirit to meet and baptise the Ethiopian eunuch (8:27–40; the Spirit is mentioned in vv. 29, 39). Deuteronomy 23:1 prevented eunuchs being fully part of the people, though Isaiah 56:3–5 spoke of a future time when God would give them a place. This follows the logic of the Samaritans – as the good news goes to another person on the edge of Judaism, the Spirit's activity makes clear that this is God's will.

Then we have the call of Paul on the road to Damascus (9:1–18). Here, Paul receives the Spirit when Ananias prays for him and lays hands on him. This is rather similar to what we have seen with the Samaritans. Ananias is not one of 'the twelve' – this isn't a special power they have – but the receipt of the Spirit does occur at the point when Paul is incorporated into the wider Christian family, as it did for the Samaritans.

The third section is the description of Peter's meeting with Cornelius, which is described in Acts 10 before being repeated in the passage we have today. The Spirit is explicitly mentioned near the beginning (10:19) and at the end (10:38, 44–45, 47), making the same point as we have in our passage.

Cornelius was a Gentile. Acts 10:2 might point out that he was a good man, but that is not important enough even to make it into Peter's telling of the story here. What matters is that he was a Gentile: unclean (vv. 1, 3, 18). If the Spirit being given to Samaritans and eunuchs was breaking the boundaries, Gentiles would be shattering them. We have already had hints that this is what God is going to do – in Jesus' own ministry (Luke 7:1–10), in the fact that the Isaiah prophecy which spoke about eunuchs went on to talk about foreigners (Isaiah 56:6–7) and in Paul's commission to go to the Gentiles (Acts 9:15). But hints are not enough for such a profound step. So, as Peter tells his story, it is made clear that the Spirit explicitly instructed him to go (v. 12) and that the decision to baptise these Gentiles was made by God himself, not by Peter (v. 15). God baptised them with the Spirit, and since that is 'higher' than water baptism, it would be silly not to baptise them and welcome them (vv. 16–17, relating back to verses 2–3). This argument wins the day (v. 19). This question of the 'uncircumcised' returns in Acts 15, where again the Spirit is explicitly seen as the key actor in the welcome offered (Acts 15:8, 28).

The Spirit is not contained by the church. He pushes ahead of it, leading the 'breaking of boundaries' and radical inclusion, just as Jesus himself did.

4 Not just crumbs

Acts 13:1–15, 44–52

Crumbs or loaves? Jesus famously accepted the argument of the Gentile woman from Syria that 'even the dogs under the table eat the children's crumbs' (Mark 7:28) and healed her child. Is this what we have? A message to the Jewish people, into which can be welcomed people on the edge of Judaism (the Samaritans and the eunuch) and a few Gentiles who get caught up on the margins? So far in Acts, this could be the interpretation.

The next step comes as the church in Antioch sends out Barnabas and Saul as what we could call missionaries. Still no mention that they are to go to Gentiles, yet 'the work to which I have called them' (v. 2) would point towards Gentiles in Paul's case, or at least a mixed mission (Acts 9:15). Nevertheless the Spirit is explicitly said to be involved – indeed it was the Spirit's idea (v. 2). Quite how the Spirit 'said' is an intriguing question, but the previous verse mentions prophets, and earlier we have read of the Spirit 'speaking through' prophets (e.g. Acts 4:25; 11:24–28). But the means is not important; what matters is that this mission was launched by the Spirit (v. 4).

The events in Cyprus have echoes both in the conversion of Cornelius and the clash with Simon the magician. The 'blockage' of Elymas the sorcerer was removed by the Spirit (vv. 8–12). It is God's will that this Gentile hears. They continue to travel away from Israel to the strategically located Roman colony of Pisidian Antioch, where they are invited to speak in the synagogue. The speech itself is well worth reading, bringing together elements of Peter's and Stephen's earlier speeches, but to track the work of the Spirit we jump to the end of the passage to see the result (vv. 44–52).

'We now turn to the Gentiles' (v. 46). This is new – a deliberate mission to the Gentiles. Loaves baked for them, not crumbs. It is emphasised and defended by the quotation from Isaiah 49:6 which says that just rescuing Israel is 'too small a thing'; God's plan is to bring salvation to 'the Gentiles' (not just the odd one). This same point is powerfully repeated at the last scene of Acts 28:23–28.

Paul and Barnabas shake the dust off their feet (v. 51) as commanded by Jesus (Luke 9:5; 10:11). Jews returning to the 'holy land' from Gentile lands would wipe off the dust from their feet to avoid polluting the promised land. For Paul and Barnabas to do this here rather implies that, by rejecting the message, the Jewish leaders in Pisidian Antioch are now 'like Gentiles', while Gentiles there have become part of God's people. The whole passage reminds us of Simeon's words that Jesus will be a light for the Gentiles and cause the falling and rising of many in Israel (Luke 2:28–35). A final mention of the Spirit filling the disciples (the converts in Pisidian Antioch in v. 52) confirms that this mission, and what then follows in Iconium (Acts 14), are God's will.

5 The Spirit guides

Acts 16:1–12

How does the Spirit guide? In one sense, this passage continues the theme we have seen since Acts 8, that key steps in the breaking of boundaries are explicitly led by the Spirit. Here, the step of moving from Asia to Europe is the work of the Spirit (vv. 6–10). Admittedly, from the point of view of Paul's day, 'western Turkey' and 'Greece' were part of the same cultural entity. But it is certainly good for Europeans in our day to note that the Spirit had to explicitly guide and confirm the mission to Europe as it had done to others 'beyond the pale'! Note in passing that the Spirit is called 'the Spirit of Jesus', verse 7; what the Spirit does is what Jesus is doing.

But how does the Spirit guide? I would love to know how the Spirit prevented Paul preaching in the province of Asia, and entering Bithynia (vv. 6–7). Perhaps this was through prophetic speech as we have seen earlier in Acts, but if it was, it is strange that it is not said openly as it has been before. If a dream or vision, why is it not described as the vision of the man of Macedonia which follows is (v. 8)? It is tempting to see the references to the Spirit here as an interpretation of circumstances, which in hindsight were seen as the work of the Spirit. We might speak of 'doors closing'. Elsewhere, Paul certainly speaks of God opening doors for his work beyond his expectations (1 Corinthians 16:9; 2 Corinthians 2:12) and in Philippians 1:12–18 he looks back on his arrest and imprisonment as surprisingly being of benefit; similarly his illness in Galatians 4:13.

This matters because we love to be in control. We are content with the idea of the Spirit guiding us, if by this we mean that the Spirit tells us the broad plan – the 'strategic direction' – and we can then take it forward using our own ideas and within our control. Indeed there are many books which look at the spread of the church in Acts and identify 'Paul's Mission Strategy', such as planting churches in key cities, and suggest that we copy it. This passage raises the possibility that it wasn't like that. God might have had a plan, but it sounds like Paul didn't know it, that he unknowingly fought against it and only in retrospect could he see that the Spirit was at work. A reminder that we work for the Spirit, not the other way round!

6 Dependent on the Spirit

Acts 20:17–35

Our last passage is Paul's speech to the Ephesian elders, in which he reflects on his missionary work and his future. Again the Spirit is prominent.

First, the Spirit is directing Paul's next steps. The Spirit, it seems, is at the same time telling Paul to go to Jerusalem (v. 22; the Greek is literally 'tied up by the Spirit'), and making clear that this will cause him great hardship. This must have been terrible. Of course, Jesus himself made clear that following him involved 'taking up our cross' and 'losing our life' (Luke 9:22–24; 14:26–27), yet it is easy for such things to be mere words; Paul is facing the reality. We get an example of the Spirit's warnings in Acts 21:4, 11. The language of tying up, suffering and handing over to the Gentiles echoes Jesus' 'passion predictions' (Luke 9:22, 33–34; 18:31–33) and the conclusion in Acts 21:14 – 'The Lord's will be done' – echoes Gethsemane (Luke 22:42).

Paul's situation is particularly hard because he doesn't actually know what will happen (v. 22), just that it won't be good (v. 23). This requires real faith and trust. There are connections here with what we saw in Acts 16. The Spirit guides, but doesn't explain the full picture or strategy.

The second reference is Paul's instruction in verse 28: 'Keep watch over yourselves and all the flock of which the Holy Spirit has made you overseers.' This is an important verse for our understanding of the emergence of leadership structures in the early church – for Paul is addressing 'elders' and calls them 'overseers' (a word which traditionally is elsewhere translated 'bishops' e.g. Philippians 1:1; 1 Timothy 3:1–7). This suggests that we should not see 'elders' and 'overseers' as distinct forms or levels of leadership (some churches see them as the origins of 'priests' and 'bishops'). We don't know how these elders were appointed. These 'elders' may be older men (as the word literally implies), and probably continues the form of governance found in synagogues. Perhaps they were 'elected'; perhaps appointed (as suggested in Acts 14:23; Titus 1:5). Our passage makes clear, though, that it is the Spirit who actually makes them overseers of God's church. The wording perhaps implies that they needed to be reminded of this; perhaps all those with responsibility in the church do. It's not our church, but God's, and whatever the processes involved, our role is dependent on the Spirit.

Guidelines

In John's Gospel, Jesus says 'the Spirit blows where he wishes' (3:8). This has been at the heart of our readings this week. The Spirit has been breaking boundaries, the Spirit removing blockages, the Spirit guiding. We are called not to resist the Spirit but to recognise our dependence on him – how might we do this?

Key is recognition – accepting that the Spirit is not a 'tool' for us to use, 'the force' for Jedi knights, 'fuel in our tank' or even 'our helper'. The Spirit is God. The Spirit is God at work in his world; the Spirit of Jesus continuing Jesus' work.

It is intriguing that we find this difficult; the starting point of Christianity is an acceptance of Jesus as Lord, a recognition of our dependence on him. But we quite like to 'move on' from that, to see that as a 'foundational truth' but not let it have too much prominence day-to-day. We will pledge our loyalty to Jesus, but still quite like to be 'in charge' of the details of our own lives. Jesus did call us 'friends' not 'servants', but even there it was 'if you do what I command' (John 15:14–15). Paul writes, 'Do not quench the Spirit' (1 Thessalonians 5:19). Our readings this week suggest a first step in this is recognising that the Spirit may be at work in new ways which we don't yet understand, and being humble enough to accept that is the Spirit's right. After all, he is God; not us. Let us pray that today, tomorrow, this week, this year, we might, in the words of Galatians 5:25, 'keep in step with the Spirit'.

Genesis 1—11

Brian Howell

The Old Testament as a whole can seem to be rather fantastical, but the first eleven chapters, or 'proto-history,' have proven more enigmatic than perhaps any other part of the Bible. This is primarily due to its content, which includes everything from a creation from nothing to global floods, astronomical human lifespans, intercourse with angels, a race of giants, talking snakes and an instantaneous origin to all human languages.

Part of the problem it presents to modern readers is the genre and context in which it is read. For example, when it speaks of origins (Latin *genesis*, Hebrew *bereshit*, 'in [the] beginning'), we tend to read this against our own debates and theories, as historical claims about when and how the world came into being, despite Darwin's *Origin of the Species* being written some 2,300–3,300 years later. However, when we compare it with contemporary ancient Near Eastern creation stories, we find accounts speaking to the function and relationship between the elements of creation, rather than simply its timescale. This, of course, does not resolve our modern debates, but does point to the fact that more is being said in Genesis than is often heard, because the questions we put to it can sometimes cause us to miss what it is really saying.

As an account of the origins of the universe, the sexes, worship, sin and languages, there is too much to be mined in this brief exploration, with nearly every word having repercussions for understanding the rest of the Bible. Hence, we will draw out some of the main issues, and some overlooked nuances as well, in the hope that we can come again to a familiar text, find more there than we have before and hopefully, hear the echo of God's voice, for it is still 'very good'.

Unless otherwise stated, quotations are from the New American Standard Bible.

1 Enraptured creator

Genesis 1:1–25, 29–31

The creation account in Genesis 1 contrasts with those from the ancient Near East in several illuminating areas. Firstly, it depicts no struggle in creation – no death of other gods or monsters required for raw materials. God speaks and instantly, effortlessly, it is so. Secondly, whereas the celestial bodies, weather phenomena and elements in the universe were deified in ancient Near Eastern stories, they are all created by God in Genesis. In fact, on day four, the typical names of the sun and moon are avoided, using rather the phrases 'greater light' and 'lesser light'. As their usual designations, *shamash* and *yereach*, were also the names of the sun and moon gods, the author emphasises that these were not divine, but created, entities.

Thirdly, we find that the days of creation are ordered to give spaces which are subsequently filled. The first day sees not only light created, but also time, as John Walton deduces from the curious use of 'day', and the alternation of evening and morning. The creation of the sky and sea follows on day two, and dry land on day three. These 'spaces' are then filled with the objects that govern time (the sun, moon and stars), the fish and fowl, and the land animals, respectively. This process of making a context and filling it builds creation towards its crowning glory – humanity – who is set to rule over it all. This contrasts starkly with the way that humans are treated as an afterthought in the ancient Near Eastern tales.

Finally, in verse 31, an unobtrusive little word reveals the relationship between the Creator and his new handiwork – 'behold'. Six times we have encountered, 'And God saw that it was good.' This time it is interrupted, building suspense, and finally resolved in a superlative conclusion. As Adele Berlin notes, 'behold' often signifies a difference in point of view where the narrative camera, once panning the scene for an overview of the action, now slips inside the head of a character to take a look through their eyes (*Poetics and Interpretation of Biblical Narrative*, pp. 62–63). Here, then, we find God himself taking in his masterpiece. He surveys all the parts, each one revealed to be genuinely, intrinsically beautiful and fit for purpose. The culmination of it all then hits him, and he smiles, like an artist stepping back to admire his *magnum opus*, finally declaring in triumph, 'very good'.

2 The spiritual image

Genesis 1:26–28

The pinnacle of creation is reached in verse 26, when God creates humanity in his image. However, what this consists of and how it is viewed has been foundational to the value and function of humanity throughout the history of Christian literature. Augustine saw it as human intelligence, rationality and freedom of choice. Karl Barth emphasised the relational element of male and female found in 1:27. Others, more recently espoused by J. Middleton's *The Liberating Image*, see the image as equivalent to humanity's function. Thus, the commands which follow verse 28 to be fruitful, multiply, fill the earth, rule over it and subdue it, are considered the image itself.

The problem with this approach is that it leaves no room for quality control. Is humanity appropriately imaging God as long as they rule over creation, even if they do so in an ungodly, tyrannical fashion? This approach conflates the function of humanity and the mechanics with which it accomplishes said function. Rather, it is because humanity is the image of God that they are enabled to image him appropriately in ruling, etc. How does this work?

In the ancient Near East, *tselem* or 'image' was one of the terms for a solid form used to represent a deity – an idol. A deity had a special relationship with its idols. They were representative of the deity, and one could point at the idol and say that the deity resided therein. On the other hand, destroying the idol did not destroy the deity, as there were many idols for the same deity, and the two were not seen as completely identical.

Idols had induction ceremonies supposedly attended by the deities they were to represent. It was only at the point when the idol was infused with the divine spirit that it was viewed as having become an official 'image' of that deity – alive and functioning. Thus, a deity's 'image' is a physical vessel for its spirit.

But what does it mean to be God's image or 'idol'? Though only Egyptian and Mesopotamian kings were called 'the image of [their] god', the Bible sees all humanity imbued with this honour, for if they are created with the intention of housing God's spirit, they too would be able to represent God's rule over creation appropriately, empowered and directed by God's own spirit to rule the earth in his uniquely wise, compassionate and gracious way.

3 A little help?

Genesis 2:1–24

Some issue is made regarding this chapter of the difference in creation order from chapter 1. The plants made on day five seem to spring up after the creation of man which was on day six. This is problematic only if one takes the purpose of chapter 1 as a chronological account of creation rather than describing the functional and relational aspects of its components, and also if one interprets chapter 2 as a wholly new account. Many interpreters rather see this as a microcosm focusing on the creation of humans and their relationship to each other, rather than the rest of creation. Indeed, regardless of how the accounts came about, the editor of Genesis certainly saw fit to juxtapose them and thus have them comment upon each other.

One striking contrast is that, unlike chapter 1, we encounter here the first instance where something in creation is said to be 'not good' – man's aloneness. Though the man names all the other creatures God brings before him, he does not find a partner suitable for himself. He finally finds the woman, the only creature not made from the dirt or sea, but from another living creature, and – bam! Finally! The woman is said to be an *ezer knegdo*, often rendered 'suitable helper'. The word *knegdo* literally means 'as before him', picturing the woman standing opposite him, and can be translated 'corresponding to'. This represents a strong case for their equality.

However, 'helper' has often signalled to English readers one who is inferior. The Hebrew word *ezer* is also used of God – in Psalm 10:14; 30:10; and 54:4 – so it does not necessarily designate someone lower in rank, status or ability. Though, as David Clines has observed, the helper, in helping, takes on a subordinate role inasmuch as the help being offered is in service of another. The responsibility still lies with the 'help-ee'. In this context, the woman is created to help the man both in fulfilling the creation mandate to 'be fruitful and multiply', but also in being a companion for him. This makes a significant statement about what is required for God-imaging relationships. The difference or 'otherness' reflects the distinction between the Father and Son within the Trinity – whereas the correspondence reflects their equality. This means the creation of woman allowed relationships to reflect that within the Trinity between different but equals (compare v. 24), and not simply as a bunch of yes-men.

4 Crime and punishment (part 1)

Genesis 2:25—3:13, 23–24

While the couple are described as 'naked (*arôm*) and unashamed', in 3:1, we find the serpent to be the 'craftiest' (*arum*) of all the creatures God had made. This subtle wordplay between the innocence of their natural state and the clever serpentine machinations foreshadows a rather more major fault line about to appear.

The serpent begins by getting the woman to question God's commands: 'Did God actually say. . .?' (v. 1, NIV) and follows by outright contradiction of God's truthfulness: 'You will not surely die!' (v. 4). Finally, he insinuates that God is paranoid, trying to keep the couple from something good he is keeping for himself. Indeed, the couple do not die immediately, as God had said, and even God agrees that they are now like him, having their eyes opened. So was the serpent right?

The serpent portrays God in increasingly draconian terms. In the original command, there is emphasis on all that is given ('from any tree of the garden you may eat freely', Genesis 2:16–17), whereas here the sole focus is the prohibition. Notably, there is no record of God giving this prohibition to the woman. This was given to the man, before the woman was created (Genesis 2:16–17). Presumably, the man relayed this command to the woman, who clearly knows of it. However, like Chinese whispers, it gets twisted in the retelling, for she adds a ban on 'touching'. Could there be a nascent Pharisaism here, safeguarding the eating by making a more sweeping prohibition? However, the serpent never tells the woman to eat – that is left entirely up to her and Adam. Adam, apparently, was 'with her' the entire time (v. 6).

What exactly was their sin? If they didn't know 'good and evil' prior to the fruit, could they have even made an ethical choice? And why would God prevent them from knowing the difference? The 'knowledge of good and evil' primarily refers to an age of accountability (e.g. Isaiah 7:15–16). However, according to Walter Moberly, the sense here is one of moral autonomy ('Did the Serpent Get It Right?', p. 24). Just as God had declared creation 'good' in chapter 1, and the man's alone-ness 'not good' in chapter 2, so here the couple decide what is good and what is not, but this time, only in relation to their own perceived desires.

5 Crime and punishment (part 2)

Genesis 3:1–24

Though God asks the couple, 'Who told you you were naked?' (v. 11), there is no record of the serpent telling them this. Nakedness was generally taboo and shameful in Hebrew society (cf. Leviticus 20:19; Job 24:7, 10; Isaiah 20:4; 58:7). However, in a land without clothes where the only residents are married to each other, to 'tell' such a person they are naked is to insinuate they 'ought' to be clothed – that there is something offensive about their natural state. While this might make sense in subsequent public situations, it did not here. The effect was that, though their state had not changed, their perception of it had. Their innocence and its outlook had been corrupted by a way of seeing the world suggested by the voice of opposition to the Creator.

Interestingly, the man alone is the first called (v. 9) to account for his actions, in reverse order of the transgressions. This signifies a greater responsibility placed upon him, perhaps because he was the only one around at the giving of the command (see Genesis 2:16–17). Despite this, he immediately shifts blame to the woman, but implicitly faults God himself ('the woman *you* gave me', v. 12). The woman, similarly, shifts it to the serpent, but there is a hint of ownership here – 'the serpent deceived me' (v. 13) – which God seems to acknowledge in the punishments – there is no 'because you have done X', as there is with the man and the serpent, and a more redemptive stance with respect to both her punishment and in her struggle with the serpent (v. 15).

In punishment, God first turns to the serpent, the root of the problem, whom he curses. Notably, God does not actually curse the man or the woman (only the ground on account of the man). But, if the punishment fits the crime, then what can it mean to be 'cursed more than all cattle', or for a snake to 'go on its belly' (v. 14)? Though its identity only becomes clearer in later scriptures (Revelation 12:9; 20:2), this strange talking serpent may be better pictured as a 'dragon' (cf. 'Leviathan' in Isaiah 27:1). If this is what was in mind, then the punishment actually represents a clipping of the serpent's wings! In any case, the creature that deceived humanity into rebelling against God undoubtedly saw itself superior to them. Its curse would render it, both physically and in jurisdiction, not only beneath humanity, but even below the beasts humanity domesticates, and thus rules.

6 Worship and wandering

Genesis 4:1–26

The stories of the proto-history have often been imagined as figurative, not representing real people. Indeed, as Gordon Wenham (*Genesis 1–15*, p. 100) observes, the parallels between Genesis 4 and Genesis 3 point toward a paradigmatic reading of the story. These similarities include: the central descriptions of sin (3:6–8; 4:8); God's enquiry concerning Adam and Abel's whereabouts; the cursing of both serpent and Cain; the grace-filled clothing of Adam and Eve and the marking of Cain; the desires of the woman to rule her husband and sin to rule Cain; and the injunctions for the latter in each case to rule the former. These parallels lead us to read the brothers as symbolic of human relations in general, and addressing the intrahuman dimension of sin.

At the same time, the differences in the stories point to reading them as real individual characters. For instance, the alienation between God and Cain at the outset is distinct from that of Adam and Eve, who initially commune with God. Whereas Eve must be tricked into disobeying God, Cain won't listen to God's pleas not to disobey. These variances, along with the differing receptions of their punishments, point to a history that has moved on, rather than unchanging ideals.

Cain is actually the first to bring sacrifice, though none is commanded. Many have wondered why God doesn't accept Cain's sacrifice; only the conspicuously enhanced description of Abel's sacrifice gives us a clue – the firstborn of the flock and the fat portions. This would certainly have connoted the best of the best to an Israelite audience.

The cry of Abel's blood is the same as those oppressed in slavery (Exodus 3:7), women being raped (Deuteronomy 22:24, 27) or people abused by their enemies (Judges 4:3). Homicide not only must be avenged (Genesis 9:6), but also defiles the land, preventing Yahweh from dwelling in it. These things are behind the rituals in Deuteronomy 21:1–9, performed even when the murderer cannot be found, and spurring the creation of cities of refuge. The fact that God hears Abel's cry affirms that he hears other such, and often wordless, cries. Cain is cursed *from* the land, that is, its produce and that of the land near Eden ('delight'); he settles in Nod ('wandering') which reminds him of this curse (see *Genesis 1–15*, p. 107).

Guidelines

Genesis 1—11 contains some of the most foundational theological material in the Old Testament. It makes us reconsider not only our origins, but also how we appropriate these texts into our current lives. Do we simply use Genesis 1 as an argument against naturalism, or can we find more of God in it? Can we join him in awe of his handiwork, both in its own right, and its integration as a whole? Are we humbled that nature and by extension all of humankind are the reflection of God?

Genesis 2 causes us to reflect on how we need others to be fulfilled, to fulfill God's calling on our lives. In what ways do we seek to complement and facilitate the gifts of others to enable them to achieve the purposes of God? Conversely, do we allow ourselves to be 'helped' – or do we stubbornly insist on going it alone? In either case, the challenge is to see God's purposes in terms of relationships as well as action.

Genesis 3 asks us, among other things, to consider our doubts about God. Do we believe he means what he says, even when circumstances do not turn out as we'd expect? What do we feel God is holding back from us? In what areas do we feel we know what's best for us?

How do we react when we are called to account? Is our first instinct to blame someone else? When might listening to others actually be taking the easy way out and disengaging from our own responsibility?

Cain and Abel present us with a few dilemmas. Do we offer the best of all that we do – not just the religious acts – to God? In what ways are we like Eve in struggling with temptation to do wrong? Where are we more like Cain in requiring (and often resisting) admonition to do right? What does this tell us about the particular bent of our hearts? Does our sense of moral rectitude stop outside the bubble that is our own life, or do we find ourselves our brother's (and sister's) keepers? What injustices might we have perpetrated that, though unseen by others, prevent the intimate and powerful presence of a holy God from being made manifest in our presence?

1 Genealogy/image

Genesis 5:1–32

Seth is said to be in the likeness of his father, Adam (v. 3), reflecting the likeness Adam bore to his father – God (v. 1), whose image he was (Genesis 1:26). However, by reversing the prepositions from the first chapter of Genesis, '*in* his likeness' becomes '*according to* his image' to avoid any claim that Seth is Adam's image (or idol). Though Seth may be the likeness of his earthly father's visage, he is the idolic vessel-image for his heavenly father's spirit.

One of the aspects of these genealogies is the long ages the original humans are claimed to have lived. With Adam living 930 years, these lists take on an air of implausibility. However, this is because we do not take into account the function of genealogies in the ancient Near East. In the Gilgamesh epic and others, similar genealogies precede the heroic tales. These lists were important, because the hero to which they lead is not worthy of admiration due to his exploits, but derives significance from where he has come. This is part of the communal identity with which modern Westerners are generally unfamiliar.

Furthermore, in the Sumerian king list, for example, the kings were said to have lived thousands of years – the Genesis account seems downright conservative in comparison, and is probably making a polemic against such lists.

The formula for grouping the accounts in Genesis, 'These are the generations of' occurs ten times (Genesis 2:4; 6:9; 10:1; 11:10, 27; 25:12, 19; 36:1, 9; 37:2). In each case, the account is about the period when the named individual is head of the clan. However, the action does not revolve around this individual, but around his sons. Hence, the 'generations of Adam' are really about Seth and his line through Noah.

Later, in the often significant seventh generation, we come across Enoch, who, because he walked with God, 'was not' (v. 24). The double mention of walking with God speaks of an extremely close relationship, and 'was not' is used for Elijah's exit in the fiery chariot, so it does seem to indicate Enoch did not die. Methuselah, Noah's grandfather, is also famous for living the longest in the biblical history, at 969 years. However, when adding up the ages from when they were born until the flood, it appears he died in the deluge. Thus, his fame does not reflect his character.

2 Sons of God and Nephilim

Genesis 6:1–4

The identity of the 'sons of God' and 'daughters of men' largely determines the meaning of the story. Three main theories have been put forward over the centuries. The first is that it represents the mixing of the 'godly' line of Seth with the 'evil' Cainite line, and the second that the 'sons of God' were early despotic rulers who so named themselves, and took whatever women they desired. These theories neither explain the large stature and fame garnered by their children, the lack of prohibition against such intermarriages, the characterisation of the two lines, nor the term 'daughters of *men*', as in each theory *both* groups would be human. The final theory, supported by the vast majority of scholars, sees the sons of God as divine beings – part of the divine council through which God ruled the universe (cf. Job 1—2; 38:7; Psalm 29:1; 82:1, 6–7; 89:6–7).

Thus, the story describes sexual intercourse between divine beings and human women, but this too raises several questions. Why are the humans punished for something done to them by divine beings? What is the point of these unions, and why include them?

Firstly, 'seeing and taking' is actually a common Hebrew expression for getting married. It does not imply force or rape – which requires a different verb. In fact, if this were the case, the protests of the women, as well as their fathers, would be expected. Their silence implies collusion, and thus punishment deserved.

Secondly, we see a parallel with Genesis 3. There too we encounter a fruit-full 'seeing and taking,' but also a supernatural being interacting directly and solely with a female and in contention with God.

Finally, the emphasis of the story is on the progeny – the Nephilim. They appear to be a race of giants, also known as the Anakim and the Rephaim from whom the infamous Goliath was descended (cf. Numbers 13:33; Deuteronomy 1:28; 2:10, 11, 21; 9:2; Joshua 11:22).

It appears that, just as the woman in the garden was seeking to have her 'eyes opened' and 'be like God', but independently of him, so here we find the daughters of men conspiring with the sons of God to achieve a sort of immortality – if not for themselves, then through their children – a sort of divine/human half-breed. This would explain why God responds by limiting human lifespans immediately after this episode and *before* the flood.

3 The righteous Noah

Genesis 6:5–22

Though some commentators see Genesis 6:1–4 as a 'nugget' placed randomly by an editor, there are many parallels and conspicuous contrasts with the following material. God sees in verse 5 the opposite of what the 'sons of God' saw. They saw that the daughters of men were literally 'good' (Geneis 6:2, often rendered 'beautiful', it is the Hebrew for 'good'), but God saw that 'the wickedness of people [including the daughters of men] was great' and the 'thoughts and intentions of their hearts were only evil continually' (v. 5).

Not only does God view things differently, but he evaluates differently. Whereas he saw what he had made according to its created purpose in chapter 1 – he took and placed the man in the garden to fulfil that purpose, and took the woman out of the man to help the couple fulfil their purposes in being fruitful and filling the earth – the sons of God take women to use for their own utilitarian and selfish purposes.

Not only does God see evil present where the sons of God only saw 'good', but he also sees evil where he once saw only good. There is no stronger statement of the complete and utter corrupted and incorrigible nature of people in the Bible than Genesis 6:5. It isn't that they got some things wrong, but were basically decent folk – they weren't even well-meaning. Not one single thought or desire was good at any moment of their lives. Evil at all times, in all ways and all places.

In verse 13, an interesting double entendre illuminates God's viewpoint of the situation. 'The end of all flesh' has come before him. Not only does this indicate what he is about to do in sending the flood, but the end of all flesh can also be seen as the trajectory or the 'road down which one is headed' and its resultant 'end'. That is, God sees where the corruption and violence into which creation has descended will lead.

But, this insight and foresight do not obscure his view, for he sees something else – the needle in the haystack. There was one who was righteous, one who is rightly related to him.

4 The flood

Genesis 7—8

In Genesis 6:9 and 11, Noah is said to be righteous and the world ruined. God acts upon what he sees – he brings the world to its end through the flood (literally 'ruins' it, Genesis 6:13), but the rightly-related he not only saves, but commits himself to them in covenant relationship. We thus do not find God acting as an arbitrary judge or vengeful monster, but simply one who responds appropriately to the free decisions of humankind.

When God 'remembers' Noah, it does not imply that he had forgotten him. As the verb typically requires a *lamed* preposition, 'to or for', it indicates not a psychological event within God, but a salvific act he performs on behalf of the one he is 'remembering' (cf. Abraham in Genesis 19:29; see also *Genesis Chapters 1–17*, p. 299). Furthermore, it wasn't Noah's righteousness, but Noah himself that God remembers. Thus, it focuses less on Noah's worthiness, but emphasises that God's deliverance came at just the right time.

The first thing Noah does after getting off the ark, after getting his 'land legs' back, is sacrifice. This is not new, but rather evidence of his general orientation to life and to God. The rising smoke is called a 'pleasing aroma' – from the same root as Noah's name – a 'rest-inducing odor' (*Genesis Chapters 1–15*, p. 308). In the Mesopotamian flood stories of Gilgamesh and Atrahasis, the gods gather around the flood survivor's sacrifice 'like flies', for they are famished. God's conspicuous lack of hunger shifts the emphasis from a divine need to a gift God wants to give. The fact that Noah is not privy to this divine self-pronouncement precludes the sacrifice from the realm of manipulative magic.

Genesis 8:21 points us to a larger question – what was the purpose of the flood, and was it effective? In Genesis 6:5, we learned that God sent the flood because of humankind's sinfulness, and here we read that he promises never again to do so, also because of humankind's sinfulness. Some authors conclude this reflects God feeling that his plan did not work – humankind did not change. However, the word *ki*, normally translated as 'because', can also be rendered 'although', which makes more sense here (*Genesis Chapters 1–15*, p. 310). In this case, *despite* humanity remaining bent to sin, God will no longer give them what they deserve, as he did with the flood. He now extends his grace, not simply to the righteous, but to all humankind.

5 A new covenant

Genesis 9:1–28

Some have seen the image of God as marred, broken or lost altogether after the fall. However, this is at odds with Genesis 9:6, which upholds the innate value of humanity, by virtue of its ongoing identification as the image of God – not only after the fall, but even after the flood.

And yet the Noahic covenant does change things. In Genesis 6:13, all flesh had corrupted its way – not just humanity. Though this may be difficult for us to picture, it can also be seen in the rainbow covenant – that God will not again bring judgement on the earth in the form of a flood. This covenant is made not only with Noah and his sons, but with the animals as well (vv. 9–10). This may provide the reason for the new provision for eating animals. Now, the fear of humankind is placed in the animals – representing a fundamental alienation of humankind from its environment. Perhaps, like Cain's sign, it is designed to prevent the newly resultant state of the world following the flood from overwhelming humanity through its acquired nature of violence.

Another conundrum in chapter 9 is the nature of Ham's sin. It seems almost unjust to modern ears to hear of him being cursed for simply laughing at his drunk, naked father. But this may not have been all that went on. Scott Hahn has made a case that it was Ham sleeping with Noah's wife – his mother (see 'Noah's Nakedness and the Curse on Canaan (Genesis 9:20–27)' with John Seitze Bergsma in *Journal of Biblical Literature* 124.1 (Spring, 2005), pp. 25–40). To uncover a man's nakedness meant to uncover his wife and sleep with her (Leviticus 18:6–8; 20:11). If this had resulted in a child, this would explain why Noah's curse landed upon Canaan, Ham's firstborn, instead of the one who had committed the offence.

The problem here lies in the other two brothers' response. Why would they back over Noah with a garment, if it was Noah's wife that Ham had 'seen' indecently? Furthermore, the response seems immediate, not a curse after a pregnancy and birth. Thus, it seems that Canaan, at least, was already born to Ham when he committed the offence against his father. As the firstborn is the firstfruit of one's body and one's heir, to curse Canaan was, in effect, to curse Ham's legacy for his disrespect.

6 Babel

Genesis 11:1–10

The post-diluvial population decides to 'make a name for themselves' by building a city and a tower whose top reaches heaven (v. 4). While this might appear innocuous to the modern reader, it was tantamount to treachery in the biblical context. This is because their settling *in one place* directly flaunted the 'creation mandate' given by their Creator to 'be fruitful, multiply and fill the earth...' (Genesis 1:28). Furthermore, the idea that they would make a name for themselves was more than simply accruing accolades for their architectural exploits. If the people at Babel represented the entire population of the world, then whom were they trying to impress? Rather than fame, it seems their project involved redefining themselves – as those who had defied their Creator, seized his power and rendered him irrelevant.

Many commentators find a hint of irony here, for to 'see the city and tower which the sons of men have built' (v. 5), God must 'go down' as this 'heaven-reaching tower' was so small. However, this conclusion may prove a bit short-sighted, for it implies that God's vision was insufficient to see the tower. Would he have had even more trouble making out its makers? Did he also need to go down to confuse their languages (v. 7)?

The clue lies in the descriptions of the location itself. In verses 4 and 5, the project is described in a repeated word pair: the 'city' and the 'tower'. Oddly, after God confuses their language, the people stop building the city (v. 8). Why not the tower as well? Because they thought they had already reached Babel, which in ancient Babylon meant 'the gate of the gods'. This would have represented independent access to the seat of power over the universe – where wars were decided, weather determined, fertility granted and wealth bestowed.

This explains why the Lord 'came down' (vv. 5, 7). Four times in verses 7–9 the little word 'there' underscores that the Lord confused their languages and scatters them – from the place to which he had gone down. If God had pronounced these same judgements from heaven, he would have implicitly conceded some measure of success to the builders – that they had indeed reached heaven! Instead, by going down to see and judge the people and their tower, God denies their audacious claim to fame, preventing them making a name for themselves. Rather, he gives them one – 'Babel' (Hebrew – 'to confuse').

The proto-history speaks not only of fantastic tales, but of the deep human need for significance. Enoch and Methuselah challenge us on what we do with our years. Will we walk with God, allowing even the mundane to be an experience of him, such that death is but a new experience of him also? A life well lived, no matter the length, is the only one worth living.

Like the 'daughters of men', though, we know we will die, and we strive for some sense of transcendence, some mark to leave on the world. What lengths we are willing to go to in order to grasp our own immortality; will we trust God to ensure our significance? The sons of God put an even finer point on it. Have we allowed our aims to recalibrate our moral compass, calling useful or even good what God sees as destructive and evil?

Sometimes, after we mess up, we feel worthless. The Noahic covenant reminds us we are still the image of God. We still can allow his spirit to direct us, thereby reflecting the true nature of his rule. Will we wallow in our self-disappointment, allowing the effects of our sin to consume even more of our lives, or press on with God anew, buoyed by the value he continues to place even in a fallen humanity? Like God, will we choose to value others, in all their fallenness, for the same reason?

The ancient Babelites allowed their technological development (bricks and mortar) to convince them they didn't need to heed or even acknowledge their Maker. Similarly, we can be lulled into the lie of chronological hubris. What knowledge, technology, modern philosophy or zeitgeist seduces us into believing that we are in total control of our lives? These can make prayer feel like a vestige of a bygone age, where people did not know as much as we think we do now.

Actually, prayer acknowledges that we neither know it all, nor even enough to make it on our own. We do not even rightly know ourselves. Our name – our renown, our legacy – does not ultimately follow from our own exploits and dreams, which often lead merely to short-sighted, short-lived achievements. Only the one residing in heaven can order our lives and give us a lasting and honourable name (Revelation 2:17).

FURTHER READING

Adele Berlin, *Poetics and Interpretation of Biblical Narrative* (Almond, 1983).
David Clines, 'The image of God in man', *Tyndale Bulletin*, 1969.
Victor P. Hamilton, *Genesis 1–17* (William B. Eerdmans, 1990).

Brian C. Howell, *In the Eyes of God: A metaphorical approach to biblical anthropomorphic language* (Pickwick, 2013).
Kenneth A. Mathews, *Genesis 1—11:26* (Broadman & Holman, 1996).
R.W.L. Moberly, 'Did the serpent get it right?' *JTS* 39 (1988), pp. 1–27.
John H. Walton, *The Lost World of Genesis One: Ancient cosmology and the origins debate* (InterVarsity, 2009).
Gordon J. Wenham, *Genesis 1–15* (Word Books, 1987).

Deliverance in the Bible

Graham Dow

'Most English ministers do not believe in evil spirits,' I said to the principal of a Chinese seminary. He laughed. Most people east of Egypt believe in evil spirits. This widespread conviction carries years of experience and challenges the predominant Western view. It is wise not to write it off as 'primitive' and unsustainable.

It is the well-known author and psychiatrist, Scott Peck, who questions why 'the concept of evil is virtually absent from psychology', in spite of 'being central to religious thought for millennia' (*People of the Lie*, p. 43). He describes from his casebook how he has been forced to see evil in some clients. He describes his observation of the ministry of deliverance in two cases.

As we approach the phenomena described in the biblical records, it is important to do so without prejudice to the way they are understood. Ninian Smart stated that for every observable phenomenon, the most appropriate categories should be developed for understanding it. If we say that all experiences of deliverance can be explained in purely psychological categories, that is reductionism and simply bad science.

As I see it, the New Testament assumption that there are real spirit entities is a credible interpretation of what was observed then and is today. As the Gospels show, the ministry of deliverance is routine.

The early church understood well that those coming to Christian faith from other faiths would carry with them spirits of false worship. All worship engages the invisible spirit realm; but only worship in Spirit and in truth is acceptable to God (John 4:24). According to the liturgies of Hippolytus, candidates for baptism from diverse religious backgrounds all received repeated deliverance right up until their baptism on Easter Day.

There is no systematic treatment in the scriptures of deliverance from evil. We must glean what we can. What I offer in these studies is largely drawn from examples in the Gospels.

Unless otherwise stated, quotations are from the New Revised Standard Version.

1 Jesus' ministry starts with deliverance

Luke 4:31–44

In the power of the Spirit (Luke 4:14), Jesus delivered the manifesto for his work at Nazareth, quoting Isaiah 61 in terms of setting free the oppressed and the captives.

Then, in the synagogue at Capernaum, his teaching on the sabbath day is astounding to his hearers in its authority. And, very quickly, a demonised man shouts out. This signifies that, from the beginning, the arrival of the kingdom of God (or of heaven) will provoke a serious battle with the powers of evil. This spiritual battle underlies the narrative of all four Gospels.

The fullest account of the man's deliverance is in Luke. It is consistent with the experience of many today who practise the ministry of deliverance.

The Greek says that the man is 'with' or 'in' a spirit of an unclean demon (v. 33). To translate this as 'possessed by' is unhelpful. It implies too great a degree of control. He just had a demon. Very few demons control us. We are not told what sin had brought this about.

The demon intends, by naming who Jesus is, to exercise control over Jesus, avoid the threat and to be left alone. The demon knows that Jesus is the 'Holy One of God' (v. 34) and that he has come to destroy evil. Notice that one demon is the speaker for the many: 'Have you come to destroy us [plural]? I know who you are.'

Jesus rebukes the demon; he commands, 'Be silent [or "be throttled"] and come out of him' (v. 35). The demon threw the man down in convulsions (Mark adds 'crying with a loud voice'); it came out of him without doing him any harm. I have heard it said that we would put the man out of the church; but Jesus put the demon out of the man.

That a man could have such a demon was not a surprise to those around. The surprise was the authority and power that Jesus showed in setting him free. That same authority and power healed Peter's mother-in-law (he rebuked the fever, v. 39). At sunset, crowds flocked to him for healing. The text here says, 'Demons *also* came out of many, shouting "You are the Son of God!"' (v. 41, my italics). It is not true, as some say, that in those days all illness was seen as caused by demons. We see here a clear distinction between healing and deliverance.

2 Deliverance is a sign of the battle with Satan

Luke 11:14–28

This passage is the most extensive teaching by Jesus of the battle he faced. To bring in the kingdom of God is a struggle of spiritual power.

Through human sin, the world has become the stronghold of Satan. He is 'the ruler of this world' (John 12:31). He offered Jesus all the kingdoms of the world if Jesus would worship him. 'The whole world is under the control of the evil one' (1 John 5:19, NIV). Jesus has come to earth to destroy the works of the devil (1 John 3:8). A bad king is not removed without a power struggle. Jesus achieves this because he is anointed by the Spirit. We must be Spirit-filled to take up this ministry.

The empire of Satan is compared to the well-defended castle of a 'strong man'. To suggest that the chief of the demons, Beelzebul, is responsible for what Jesus accomplishes (v. 15) is ridiculous; a divided house cannot stand (vv. 17–18). Jesus' enemies are clutching at straws.

Deliverance was practised by Jewish exorcists with long incantations. 'They will be your judges,' says Jesus (v. 19). Only Jesus dealt with demons solely in his personal authority. If Jesus is casting them out 'by the finger of God' (v. 20), this shows that the kingdom of God has come. Jesus' healings indicate emphatically that God loves to heal; for, in Jesus, 'the whole fullness of deity dwells bodily' (Colossians 2:9). We see in Jesus at one and the same time both what God is like and what we can be like.

The demon cast out in this story was a demon of dumbness ('blind and mute', Matthew 12:22). Demons can cause any kind of disorder. We read of a spirit of infirmity, a bent back (Luke 13:11), a dumb and epileptic spirit (Mark 9:17–18). There are similar healings which are just healings; no spirit is mentioned.

The passage continues with an enigma. A person has been made clean, yet the demon returns with others. This is a warning – it is not sufficient to get the demon out; Christ must take his rightful place at the centre of our being. We are then transferred from the kingdom of darkness to the kingdom of Christ (Colossians 1:13). If we are confident in Christ at the centre of our lives, then our protection stands against any further inroads of the enemy.

3 Mental illness and the enigma of the pigs

Luke 8:26–39

This is a difficult story. The man is very seriously mentally ill. The normal word in the Gospels for a demon is *daimonion*: a diminutive, 'a little demon'. This man had many – 'Legion'. Matthew uses the stronger word *daimon*. For once, the word 'possession' might be appropriate.

Our thought processes are fragile and easily disturbed. Since evil spirits can reinforce any kind of disorder, it is my personal view that, in some cases of mental illnesses, there is a potential deliverance aspect. Deliverance in no way removes a person's responsibility by blaming a spirit, as some allege. Personal responsibility is absolutely necessary: should the demons leave, the person will only be free if they have learned to exercise their will to think and act rightly. Rebuilding someone's broken will is often the much more challenging task.

The demons are very afraid and want to be left alone. The leading demon shouts out who Jesus is and begs not to be tormented. It says that Jesus had commanded the unclean spirit to come out (v. 29). Perhaps thus far he had not succeeded. He asks the demon its name; occasionally this is important to discover the identity of the spirit. The words 'evil spirits' and 'demons' are used interchangeably. The demons (plural) repeatedly beg Jesus not to order them into the abyss. They know that there they will one day be destroyed.

The demons wanted to enter the pigs to avoid destruction in the abyss. Why did Jesus let them enter? Jews were not allowed to keep pigs. But this was Gentile territory. Was Jesus wanting to get them out of the way so that they could not return to the man or destroy someone else? Was it to do with the water, where some spirits were believed to reside? Was it to make the Gentiles ask, 'Who is this?' and to show the power of Israel's God? We don't know.

The episode caused great fear among the people. We too fear what we cannot control. If we are to share in Jesus' healing and deliverance ministry, we have to be at ease with the Holy Spirit's power. Like wind, it is usually gentle, but sometimes a gale. The man was told to remain behind in the community as a sign of the wonderful good which Jesus had achieved in the power of God.

4 Deliverance requires faith and prayer

Mark 9:14–29

The disciples had seen Jesus do many acts of deliverance. Seventy had returned joyfully from a mission saying, 'Lord, in your name even the demons submit to us' (Luke 10:17). Jesus said, 'See, I have given you authority to tread on snakes and scorpions, and over all the power of the enemy, and nothing will hurt you. Nevertheless, do not rejoice at this... but rejoice that your names are written in heaven' (Luke 10:19–20). We must beware of the idolatry of success in our ministry.

In today's reading, a man has brought his dumb, deaf and epileptic son to the disciples for deliverance and it hasn't happened. Jesus, descending from the Mount of Transfiguration, is brought down to earth and, in a rare expression of emotion, expresses his exasperation at the lack of faith he finds.

'How long has this been happening?' (v. 21) is a useful question. Was the condition inherited, or gained through an event in the person's life? 'From childhood' suggests the former. Inherited spirits are the hardest to shift. Those which enter during a person's lifetime normally go with confession and repentance.

Faith has several important aspects. There is the faith of the minister, in this case the disciples with insufficient faith, and there is the faith of the community. Jesus could not do many mighty works in Nazareth because of unbelief in their local boy (Mark 6:5–6).

Thirdly, there is the faith of those coming for healing. Jesus never sends anyone away as having insufficient faith; but on several occasions, he says that the person's faith has brought the cure.

The father's faith looks weak: 'If you are able to do anything, have pity on us and help us' (v. 22). This is a weak faith environment for the disciples' failed attempts. Faced with quite a battle of faith, Jesus, in uncharacteristically strong words, rebukes the unclean spirit: 'You spirit that keep this boy from speaking and hearing, I command you, come out of him, and never enter him again' (v. 25). There is a shriek, and the boy appears to be dead. Jesus lifts him up; and we assume that he could now speak and hear.

The disciples were surprised at their failure. Jesus tells them that 'this kind can only come out through prayer' (v. 29); some versions add, 'and fasting'. The only way through the harder healings is a willingness to seek God in faith and prayer.

5 When evil spirits reinforce wrong behaviour

1 Samuel 18:6–16

The Old Testament assumes that spirits exist, but gives them little attention.

There are three occasions on which it is said that 'an evil spirit from God' or 'from the Lord' came upon King Saul. The first follows Saul's clear disobedience to God's commands (1 Samuel 16:14). Saul failed to wait for Samuel to come before offering sacrifices, and he failed to follow God's instructions for the destruction of Amalek. Despite the Spirit of God making him a new person, with a new heart (1 Samuel 10:6–13), rebellion had gone to Saul's head.

The second occasion, in our reading today, follows David's famous victory over Goliath. Women sing, 'Saul has killed his thousands, and David his ten thousands' (v. 7). Saul was angry and jealous; he said, 'What more can he have but the kingdom?' (v. 8). From that day on, Saul envied David.

The next day, an evil spirit from God came upon Saul and, while David was playing the lyre, Saul threw a spear at him. What began as anger and jealousy becomes attempted murder.

By the third occasion, Saul is intent on killing David (1 Samuel 19:9–17). He is driven for many years by the desire to pursue and kill him. David frequently evades Saul's pursuit, and steadfastly refuses to take Saul's life. Saul, he says, is 'the Lord's anointed'.

Here we see that, when we hold on to a wrong attitude, it opens the door to an evil spirit. The right of the spirit to enter us is given by our deliberate sin, our wrong attitude. The spirit holds us captive; it becomes very difficult to change our behaviour. To get free, confession of the sin which gave the spirit access is necessary, often in the presence of a Christian leader.

God is not evil. He has allowed what Saul has brought upon himself by his evil choices. It is true that our 'adversary the devil prowls around, looking for someone to devour' (1 Peter 5:8). Where sin is embraced, God allows the spirits to enter. 'An evil spirit from God' (v. 10) is simply shorthand.

This may be controversial, but it is my personal experience that to cling to a wrong attitude such as lying, anger, rebellion, hate, unforgiveness, lust or rejection is an invitation for Satan to lock you into those attitudes with an evil spirit.

6 Faith and persistence

Matthew 15:10–31

What corrupts us is not neglect of food laws or ritual hand-washing. Jesus' teaching reinforces yesterday's argument that what corrupts us is the wrong attitudes we hold and the outworking of these in words or actions. Jesus gives a list of attitudes which, if we cling on to them, easily invite the devil's attention.

In the following story of the Canaanite woman, the woman's daughter is not present. This is deliverance at a distance.

The Gospel writers love to describe outsiders as examples of faith to the nation of Israel. Jesus' reputation has reached the boundaries of Israel, and this Gentile woman will not be denied. Like the man with leprosy (Matthew 8:1–2) and the Roman centurion (Luke 7:1–10), she knows that Jesus has the power to meet what she needs.

Jesus initially states his mission to be only to 'the lost sheep of the house of Israel' (v. 24; see also Matthew 10:5–6). Israel's hopes at that time were for a messiah who would deliver Israel from Roman occupation; no Gentile mission was in view. Nevertheless, God's purpose all along was for blessing through Israel to all the nations. Simeon's words in Luke 2:29–32 speak of the child Jesus bringing the light of salvation not only to Israel but also to the Gentiles (see also Isaiah 49:6).

So is Jesus' exclusive mission to Israel just the first stage? Or is he teasing the woman to draw out her faith? She understood that the Jews considered the Gentiles as dogs. Her reply looks like a Holy Spirit-given 'word of wisdom'. She refuses to take personal offence; her persistence is admirable. Real faith has persistence. 'Faith is the assurance [Greek, *hupostasis*] of things hoped for' (Hebrews 11:1). Certainly, for this woman, what she hopes for has already happened in her mind.

Jesus does not hesitate to speak of degrees of faith. This woman has 'great faith'. He knows that the woman's faith has made it certain. Jesus need not even call on the Spirit's power; he just announces that her request is granted.

It is unwise to put limits on what God will do, for example if we are asked to pray for someone who is not present or not a believer. Maybe the Spirit will show us what our faith or the faith of others will deliver. Nothing is too hard for the Lord.

Guidelines

- In what ways have these studies opened up for you new lines of thought?
- In our culture, the existence of evil spirits is dismissed and few Christians have personal experience of deliverance ministry. How would you express your own personal thoughts on the matter? If, like Scott Peck, you have experienced something like the deliverances described in the Gospels, do you think it might alter your understanding?
- I wrote in my introduction that 'most people east of Egypt believe in evil spirits'. How do you respond? Has the West something to learn?
- How would you describe evil spirits and what are they? Is the best understanding that they are fallen angels (Revelation 12:9; Jude 6)?
- If we reject belief in demons, should angels have to go as well? They are 'ministering spirits sent to serve those who will inherit salvation' (Hebrews 1:14, NIV). Angels feature over 300 times in scripture; the biblical history cannot be written without them. I have met many people with authentic angel stories today. I have also seen many people set free of demons.
- Do you think a Christian can have a demon? Christ is at our centre; but we know that sin still lurks within us. If holding wrong attitudes can bring demons, may they still lurk in believers?
- What is your reaction to the early Christian church repeatedly exorcising those coming from backgrounds in other religions? Do you think false worship could bring spirits of deceit?

FURTHER READING

Graham Dow, *Explaining Deliverance* (Sovereign World, 2012).
Peter Horrobin, *Healing Through Deliverance* (Sovereign World, 2008).
Francis MacNutt, *Deliverance from Evil Spirits* (Chosen Books, 2009).
M. Scott Peck, *People of the Lie* (Arrow Books, 2006).
Graham Twelftree, *Christ Triumphant: Exorcism then and now* (Hodder, 1985).

Mark 4:1—6:29

Steve Motyer

Back to Mark! We land in the second main division of Mark's narrative (3:20—6:6), which focuses on *Jesus' identity*. Though Mark announces who Jesus is at the start (1:1), he then tells the story as if to seek to convince his readers of this: or more exactly, as if his bold description, 'Son of God', needs to be unpacked and explored. What exactly does it mean to describe Jesus as 'the Son of God'?

Our readings cover the four parables (4:1–34) and four miracles (4:35—5:43) with which Mark begins to provide an answer. In a nutshell, he shows how Jesus as the Son of God *speaks the word of God* (the four parables) and *acts with the power of God* (the four miracles). But this is too simple, for the words that Jesus speaks are parables, nothing like the prophetic 'oracles' with which people were familiar from those who previously spoke the word of God. Why 'parables'? Mark will say that parables, as a form of teaching, fit with the arrival of the kingdom of God in Jesus – but how?

And when it comes to the miracles, Mark tells four fascinating stories that highlight the need for faith, in different ways. We discover that it's a prerequisite – miracles can't happen without faith (5:34, 6:5). But not always: the poor demonised man in 5:1–20 ends up believing, but before the miracle he is incapable of faith; and the miracle in 4:35–41 happens because the disciples don't believe enough. We discover that it is possible to trust Jesus without really knowing who he is, like the disciples heading out on their first mission (6:7–13). And we will notice how amazingly private the miracles are: experienced by the disciples only (4:35–41), by a terrified man and a few Decapolis swineherds (5:1–20), by a tormented woman who can only assert her healing (it isn't obvious to all – 5:25–34), and by two parents who end up unsure exactly what Jesus has done (5:35–43). Jesus' miracles are not meant to convince sceptics, but – just like the parables – to picture and convey the power of the kingdom to those who are already stepping into it. Sceptics, like the swineherds and the inhabitants of Nazareth (6:1–6), simply decline the invitation.

Quotations are from the New Revised Standard Version, although occasionally I have used my own translation.

1 The master's voice

Mark 4:1–9

At last we get to hear Jesus! Mark has frequently told us about Jesus' teaching (1:21; 2:1, 13, etc.), underlining its amazing, crowd-pulling impact (e.g. 1:27), and emphasising that his preaching and teaching is the whole purpose of his mission (1:38–39) – but we've only actually heard brief summaries of his message, like 1:15, or titbits like 2:19–22 and 3:23–27. What would we hear if we stood with that 'very large crowd' (v. 1) on the shore to hear him teach from a boat? Mark 4:1–32 gives us the second-longest connected piece of Jesus' teaching in Mark (the longest is 13:5–37) – and what a surprise it is.

Jesus did not give the crowd anything remotely like what we would call a 'sermon'. 'He taught them many things in parables,' says Mark (v. 2), later telling us that Jesus 'did not speak to them except in parables' (4:34). The description 'parable' can cover proverbs or wisdom sayings, metaphors, illustrations, allegories – in fact any kind of figurative language which seeks to make truth vivid and impactful. But – amazingly – Jesus' parables usually say nothing about the truth they seek to convey. They just give the picture, and leave people with the challenge to 'listen!' (v. 3): 'if you have ears to hear, then hear!' (v. 9).

He simply invites people to listen, and then to ask themselves, 'Why is Jesus telling this story? What does it mean?' He leaves open not only people's response to the message, but also their understanding of the message to which they respond. In fact our mental and imaginative impression of any 'message' is already the first stage of our response to it. And that, of course, seems to be what the parable of the sower is about – doesn't it? Different types of response to the word of God, represented as the sowing of the seed in different areas of the field? Ignoring Jesus' explanation in 4:14–20, what would be your response to this parable, if you were standing at the water's edge listening? Where do you feel yourself drawn by it – both emotionally and cognitively? Which element in the story touches you most deeply?

Quite apart from the message each of us hears for ourselves, there is much for the church to learn from Jesus' method about how to present the good news today. How should we do it?

2 Indoors with Jesus

Mark 4:10–12

Surprisingly, Mark breaks off his presentation of Jesus' public teaching and takes us indoors with 'those who were around him along with the twelve' (v. 10). They ask what Mark's readers must have been asking – 'Why parables? And what do they mean?'

In his reply, Jesus does two things. First he distinguishes between two audiences – those with him now, and 'those outside' – and says that the parables are for the latter, while those on the inside receive 'the mystery of the kingdom of God'. We would be wrong, I think, to assume that 'the mystery of the kingdom of God' is just the explanation of the parables in non-parabolic language: this is part of it (see 4:13–20), but Jesus uses parabolic language even within his explanation (e.g. 'bear fruit' in 4:20), and then tells another string of parables just for these insiders (4:21–25)! Rather, 'mystery' points to God's secret council, to which 'his servants the prophets' are admitted, according to Amos 3:7 – the place where God reveals his mind and heart to those called to hear it. And of course *Jesus himself* is that secret, in Mark's Gospel: he is the 'mystery of the kingdom of God', because the kingdom in some amazing way arrives with him (see Mark 1:15).

Secondly, Jesus quotes Isaiah 6:9–10 to explain why he uses parables for 'those outside'. At first sight this doesn't seem to help at all, for the passage apparently says that the parables are meant to obscure the truth, to stop 'those outside' from truly seeing, understanding and finding forgiveness. But that can't be right! How could this fit with the appeal in Mark 1:15?

The context in Isaiah is important. Isaiah 6 describes how Isaiah was called to be a prophet, admitted to God's secret council and given a terrible mission to Israel, one which he is told will be completely unsuccessful: his preaching will simply serve to harden people's minds (Isaiah 6:10). Isaiah was later mocked for using simplistic 'baby' language (Isaiah 28:9–10), so his attempts to make the message as simple and clear as possible backfired. This is Jesus' reason for using parables, I believe: they may confirm people in their non-comprehension, but essentially they are a means of *clarity*, not *obscurity*, seeking to capture people with imagery that will make them question, and thus draw them gently 'indoors with Jesus'. A great place to be!

3 Jesus on his own parable

Mark 4:13–20

Can the parables have a right or wrong interpretation? I imagine someone in that indoor seminar saying to Jesus, 'Rabbi, when you talked about the seed being choked by brambles I immediately thought of poor Israel, strangled by the Romans and their armies! And when you spoke of the good seed bearing fruit in the good soil – well, thank God for our Pharisees who study to live so faithfully and who will reap the glorious harvest of their fruitfulness on the last day!' Would Jesus say 'Sorry – that's not right', when he has explicitly left the interpretation open for people to 'hear' what strikes them (vv. 3, 9)?

Yet he offers his own 'reading' (or 'hearing') of the parable here, which – in contrast to my imaginary disciple above – casts *himself* in the role of the sower (rather than God), and makes his kingdom preaching the seed (rather than the law). He is the 'mystery of the kingdom of God', after all! This is the extra, hidden secret which he wants his disciples to grasp.

Clearly Jesus (and Mark) sees the sower as 'a parable about the parables', a picture of his whole ministry. Hence the introductory comment in verse 13. From Paul we are familiar with the trio 'the world, the flesh and the devil' as a summary of the enemies of faith with which we wrestle (e.g. Ephesians 2:2–3); we meet the same trio here, as Jesus pictures what can prevent and undermine a deep response to his word. It's a tragic story:

1. In and out (v. 15): the devil will use every possible means to distract people immediately from the word – the quicker the better.
2. A little longer (vv. 16–17): it's so hard to maintain faith if the world around calls you a fool – even if you start with great enthusiasm.
3. Almost the real deal (vv. 18–19): the word lasts for even longer here, but finally the legitimate concerns of our fleshly existence simply choke its growth in our hearts. Wealth 'deceives' (not 'lures') by speaking its own word of assurance, very different from Jesus' word.

But there is the possibility of living a truly fruitful life, if the message and the mystery of the kingdom of God – Jesus Christ himself – take root in our hearts and transform us (v. 20). What might that look like for you?

4 Sound judgement: a great prize

Mark 4:21–25

We need sound judgement for every opinion and decision we form or take. It is true that our judgements impact our relationships and create an environment around us – or as Jesus puts it, 'the measure you use on others will be the measure they use on you, with more added!' (v. 24, my translation).

Why are these verses here? 'And he said to them' (v. 21) suggests that, in Mark's mind, Jesus continues to speak to the indoor seminar. But what is the connection of thought between this passage and verses 10–20? A little thought reveals it – prompted by noting the difference between Mark's version of the saying in verse 21 and Matthew's. In Matthew 5:15 onwards, the same saying is about *us*: we mustn't hide our light under a 'bushel basket', but let our good works shine before others. But here the lamp 'comes', reminding us of Jesus 'coming' to fulfil his mission (cf. Mark 1:7, 24, 39; 2:17; the NRSV 'is brought' loses this link). So Jesus the light has 'come' not to be hidden, but to shine – and yet at the moment he *is* hidden, withdrawn 'indoors' with his disciples. Why? He assures them that there is a purpose here: the withdrawal is 'so that' the hidden may 'come to light' in due course (v. 22).

The purpose is revealed in verses 23–25. It's all about the training of his disciples. Jesus repeats his public appeal of 4:9, 'let anyone with ears to hear listen!' (v. 23), because even on the inside we need ears tuned to the wavelength of the kingdom, if we are to hear its message. But on the inside, we can take steps to sharpen our hearing: 'take care over what you hear!' (v. 24). This means more than 'pay attention to what you hear' (NRSV), as though Jesus was simply telling them to stop looking out of the window. He's asking them to critique their hearing – to be aware of how much their 'hearing' of the word is shaped by their own ideas and instincts, so that they hear what they expect or want. The parallel in Luke 8:18 says even more sharply, 'take care over *how* you hear'.

Our capacity to hear the word truly will shape all our judgements (v. 24), and open up a wonderful path of growth for us (v. 25a). Or possibly not (v. 25b).

5 The kingdom of God is as if...

Mark 4:26–29

Today and tomorrow we read two 'parables of the kingdom' which Mark adds, giving the impression that Jesus is now outside again with the crowd. That is what his conclusion suggests, in verses 33–34, and the simple introduction here, 'and he said' (v. 26), supports this thought. But it's not clear. Why does Mark blur the distinction between inside and outside, having made it so sharply in verse 11? The fact is, those 'inside' face exactly the same challenge as those 'outside' – to have 'ears to hear' what the parables say. The difference is simply that those 'inside' are closer to Jesus, and they question and seek, and seem to *want* to have 'ears to hear'. In terms of the parable of the sower, they are past stage one – Satan has not snatched the seed away – so that outcomes two, three and four are now possible for them. Which will it be?

What do you 'hear' when you read this parable about the seed growing by itself? Free yourself from the quest for a 'right' interpretation, and simply let your ear hear whatever it might say to you about God's kingdom. What comes up for you? Which bit of the imagery strikes you most strongly, and why? Allow a little space to do this.

My reflections might not be yours. But I'm struck by the contrast between this parable and the sower. There is no mention of failed growth here, but in contrast a sense of inevitable progress, under God's invisible supervision. He gives the growth, which just happens automatically (v. 28), without any obvious direct intervention from him. I want to apply this to myself and my love for God and understanding of him – he will grow me to maturity! I also want to apply it to my children (for two of them, their faith is very much underground at the moment), and to the whole church of Jesus Christ, so fractious and disjointed in its growth and in its shrinkage in the world today: how great to apply to it this image of God's patient superintendence, slowly but inevitably leading us towards the final harvest!

Elsewhere, we learn that the church must work to 'build itself up in love', as Paul puts it in Ephesians 4:16. But the message here is – just sit back, take yourself off to bed and let God get on with it. How encouraging.

6 Kingdom shelter

Mark 4:30–34

This parable begins with two questions which invite us to join in (v. 30). So what picture would you decide upon, to 'capture' the reality of the kingdom of God? The second question is literally, 'In what parable should we place it?' – as if a parable is a kind of container, and the search is for the best one to hold the kingdom of God.

Jesus then (presumably) gives us *his* best shot – his best candidate for a parable to hold the kingdom. Or at least, Mark chooses for us, from the many available (see v. 33), the parable which he thinks best 'contains' the kingdom. Again, what does this parable of the mustard bush say to you? What questions does it provoke for you? If you could go indoors with Jesus after hearing this, what would you ask? What feeling does it create in you?

Whatever it says to us, our 'hearing' can be supported by thinking about some features of the picture. The mustard seed was proverbially the smallest of all seeds, and the plant in mind is probably the mustard shrub which could grow quickly to six to eight feet – certainly big enough for birds to shelter in it. One of the major points of the parable is therefore the contrast between tiny, almost invisible beginnings and wonderful, impactful outcomes.

There may also be a political overtone here in the picture of the birds sheltering, because of the Old Testament imagery lurking in the background. 'Birds sheltering in trees' could just be a picture of God's wonderful ordering and provision, as in Psalm 104:12, but it is also a not uncommon image for the shelter a great kingdom can give for smaller nations – Assyria (Ezekiel 31:3, 6), Babylon (Daniel 4:12, 21), and Israel herself (Ezekiel 17:23). Maybe we should be reminded of the vision in Daniel 2, where 'the God of heaven shall set up a kingdom that shall never be destroyed' (Daniel 2:44), filling the earth and displacing all the mighty empires that have preceded it. It's an image of wonderful strength offering a home to the vulnerable.

What does it say to us today? I leave that to you to decide.

Guidelines

What surprises Mark 4 has sprung on us! At last we get to hear Jesus' teaching, but instead of prophetic denunciation of injustice (like Amos), or dark prediction of coming judgement (like Jeremiah), or powerful proclamation of God's salvation (like Isaiah), or of his glory (like Ezekiel) or his love (like Hosea), we get *parables*: and clearly this is no random choice of method by Jesus, but rests on a conviction – shared obviously by Mark – that this is the appropriate way in which to announce the coming of the kingdom of God. It is truly amazing that parables are Jesus' core teaching method (4:34) – a method that seeks to inspire the imagination and provoke a search, rather than dictate content.

Why is this? Reflect for a moment on what answer you would give to this question. Why parables?

And what do you think of the answer given to precisely this question in Mark 4:10–12?

The fact is that people are indeed divided between those who feel little attraction to Jesus, and those for whom the story and stories of Jesus hold much power. Or maybe it would be more true to think of a spectrum here, with people spread along it from 'complete disinterest' at one end to 'deep fascination' at the other.

Where do you sit on that spectrum?

Reflect back on your reactions to the parables we have read this week. What are you left with? What questions are bubbling for you? What would you really like to ask Jesus for, right now?

And how is the word doing in the soil of your life, given all the possible obstacles to its growth (4:17–19)?

You would not be reading these notes if you were not part of the 'inner' group to whom the 'mystery' of the kingdom of God is given (v. 11). Turn that thought into prayers of thankfulness and hope.

1 In the face of the storm

Mark 4:35–41

Jesus' words and his actions carry the same authority – we saw this in 1:27: the authority of the kingdom of God. So now, after four parables, Mark records four miracles (4:35–5:43), which *display* the kingdom power of God in action just as the parables have *pictured* it. And underlying it all is the question the disciples ask in verse 41, 'Who then is this?' This is the question that underlies this whole section of the Gospel, beginning with the Pharisees' identification of his authority with that of the devil in 3:22. Whose power is it by which Jesus commands a storm to cease? And how does he come to be wielding that power at his own wish?

There is more to this story than meets the eye, too. Raging waters, in the Bible, often represent the powers of evil and of chaos that rage against God and his people, from which monsters arise (see Daniel 7:3): but at the same time God 'made the sea and the dry land' (Jonah 1:9), as Jonah confesses to his fellow-sailors, giving them the reason why *he* is the cause of the storm threatening to sink the ship in which he was trying to escape from that very God. Psalm 46:1–3 expresses beautifully God's rule over these raging waters. Trusting in that God, here in Mark Jesus sleeps through the storm (v. 38).

Here's an amazing paradox! If the disciples had had the same faith – the faith Jesus gently chides them for not having (v. 40) – the miracle would not have happened. They would have come through fine, albeit wet and exhausted. They would not have fallen into terror and woken Jesus with their frantic accusation, 'Do you not care that we are perishing?' (v. 38). This miracle happens not in response to faith, but because of *lack* of faith, and Jesus' gracious response to the disciples' fear.

Miracles have a 'parabolic' quality in Mark – they carry messages, like the parables. Here the sea could symbolise whatever 'monster' might be causing us to scrabble around in desperation, trying to escape. Even if there is no miraculous 'stilling of the storm' for us, we still have a God who 'made the sea' and whose power, therefore, will keep us safe through the darkest tempest. If we panic, he may not still the storm as here, but for sure he will pick up a bucket alongside us!

2 Stilling more storms (1)

Mark 5:1–13

We spend two days with this powerful story, looking at it from two perspectives – the personal and the political. The personal, of course, is the more obvious: here is a terribly sick man, whose dreadful psychosis is caused by a demon. He exists in a mania of self-harm and violent antisocial behaviour, cut off from human society and living beyond restraint in a graveyard. No one 'has the strength' to subdue him (v. 4). This is extreme mental illness, allied in his case to dreadful spiritual oppression by the powers of evil.

Into his world steps the 'Stronger Man' – remember the little parable in 3:23–27? 'No one can enter the strong man's house and plunder his goods, unless he first binds the strong man. Then he can plunder his house!' (3:27). The stilling of the storm by the power of Jesus' word is followed by another 'stilling' – another subduing of the powers of evil that hold this poor man in their grip. 'Come out of the man, you unclean spirit!' (v. 8).

The mental and the spiritual go so closely together. Actual demon possession, requiring exorcism, seems to be less common now in Western cultures, though still widely encountered elsewhere. But those who suffer mental anguish have no difficulty in identifying the demonic in their experience – especially in the derogatory, lying, cruel messages that so many experience within them, often as real voices in the mind. Such voices seem so powerful, shouting down grace, mercy and truth in a barrage of hostility and scorn.

There is of course healing to be gained through psychological therapies of many sorts: and all of them seek to strengthen an inner message of mercy, love and truth so that it can combat these other voices. These therapies simply act on behalf of the one who is truly the Stronger Man, and whose voice can speak peace and restoration in a moment, by his powerful grace. He is the agent of God's kingdom mercy (look ahead to 5:19), speaking a word of command that transforms in an instant. One moment, tortured beyond imagination. The next, 'clothed and in his right mind' (5:15). What a prize the kingdom of God brings, and offers still! Most need to grow slowly to health, but the end (mental wholeness) and the means (God's kingdom, active in the world) is always the same as for this man.

3 Stilling more storms (2)

Mark 5:1–13

There's more! This story has an unmistakable *political* message, too. Israel at this time was under enemy occupation by the Romans, who had overrun the whole area, even this distant bit of land on the eastern side of Galilee which was really outside the official borders of Israel. The Romans were 'unclean' invaders, whom many longed to expel from the Holy Land. So when the unclean spirits in this man call themselves 'Legion' (v. 9), and 'beg him repeatedly not to send them out of the land' (v. 10, my translation), the political overtones are clear. The 'legion' was the basic unit of the Roman army, containing 6,000 men at full complement, but often less than that. This 'legion' musters 2,000 (v. 13) – an entire regiment in one poor man! Jesus permits the unclean spirits to stay in the land, but they must go where they belong – first into the pigs, unclean animals, and then into the sea, the place of chaos and the powers of evil (v. 13).

The point is that the personal and the political go together, because this is God's *kingdom* in action. As in Daniel's visions of God's kingdom, which lie behind Jesus' proclamation, God's kingdom is the greatest of all, and comes ultimately to displace the kingdoms of the world. See especially Daniel 2 and 7 if you'd like to follow this up. The vision in Daniel 2 lies behind the powerful vision in Daniel 7 on which both Jesus and the Gospel-writers draw for their understanding and proclamation of the kingdom of God. It's an intensely political vision, about the rescue of God's people from the powers that have been oppressing them (see especially Daniel 7:25–27). That is exactly what Jesus does for this man – on a much grander scale than mere political deliverance.

God's kingdom reaches out with love and healing, ruling not by oppression (like the Romans) but by compassion. It is not a political movement, opposing the powers of this world on their own turf. Rather, it's a mysterious otherworldly rock knocking them over and growing to fill the whole world (Daniel 2:34–35, 44–45). It's a light shining, a crop growing quietly and mysteriously, a mustard shrub suddenly big enough to shelter the weak like this man (4:21–32). That's the kingdom of our Lord Jesus Christ!

4 So much! – No, too much!

Mark 5:14–20

Mark vividly pictures reactions to the healing – first that of the locals (vv. 14–17), then that of the demonised man himself and the wider region (vv. 18–20).

The locals rush to the scene, and, when they see the demonised man 'sitting, clothed and in his right mind', Mark tells us 'they were afraid' (v. 15). Mark often describes 'fear' as the first reaction to the presence or power of God (see, for example, 6:50, 10:32 and especially 16:8). It's the fear of something awesome, beyond our control, overwhelming, deeply disturbing – all the things the kingdom of God is! And therefore we are forced to decide: do we want this? Can we cope with the disturbance?

The locals then learn about the pigs (v. 16), and quickly decide that they can't cope with it: 'They began to beg Jesus to leave their neighbourhood' (v. 17). Would they prefer 2,000 pigs, or the demonised man healed? There's no argument – they prefer the pigs. They can't risk this happening again. There is huge irony in their 'begging' Jesus to leave; the demons likewise 'begged' Jesus not to expel them, and he let them stay, in the pigs (vv. 10–13). But *he himself is therefore thrown out*, because the demons stayed in the land and the pigs were lost. This foreshadows the cross – Jesus' rejection and execution at the hands of the earthly kingdom authorities, both Roman and Jewish. One man, naked and tortured among the tombs, is finally restored to himself and his family because one day another will be stripped naked, tortured and hung out to die.

The demonised man wants to join the disciples (v. 18), but Jesus tells him instead to go home and tell his family 'how much the Lord has done for you, and the mercy he has shown you' (v. 19). How different from Jesus' gagging order in 1:44! But if Jesus meant 'just your family', then, like the leper in 1:45, this new man can't keep the restriction: 'He began to proclaim in the Decapolis [this whole area, abutting the south-east shore of Galilee] how much Jesus had done for him' (v. 20). He becomes the first missionary!

This disturbing story makes us ask in what ways the kingdom of God is unacceptable to us: where is it too disturbing, too demanding, too uncomfortable? Or else we ask: what experience of healing would be too great to keep silent about?

5 Two desperate people

Mark 5:21–28

Miracles three and four in this sequence of four stories are told in a 'Markan sandwich', with one wrapped inside the other. It's a favourite technique of Mark's – we met it already in 3:21–35, and there is a long sandwich in the next chapter (6:7–32). See also – famously – 11:12–25, where the stories of the cursing of the fig-tree and the cleansing of the temple intertwine. In all these cases, the two stories soak into each other, generating contrasts and comparisons, and shared themes.

Today we meet the two main actors in these dramas, both finding their way to Jesus. How different they are! Jairus is a 'community leader', a man of status and significance, known to all. The crowd parts as he pushes through, until he sees Jesus and abandons his dignity by falling at his feet. It is so easy to feel his pain with him, and his hope as he brings his fear and faith to Jesus, the great healer.

The excited crowd presses around as Jesus sets off slowly with Jairus (v. 24). So no one makes way for the other significant figure here. No one sees her, or even senses the gentle pressure of her arms and shoulders as she squeezes through, trying to get close enough to Jesus to touch his cloak. But how significant her touch is! She is unclean, suffering from persistent bleeding. According to the purity laws, she infects everyone she touches with her uncleanness. What a risk she takes, trying to squeeze through the crowd unnoticed! Normally she keeps well away, and people avoid her. But she is desperate for release, and animated by a glorious hope, and faith: 'If I can touch even just his clothes, I'll be saved!'

Different though they are, these are two deeply 'human' figures, with stories that touch the experience of all. We may never see a storm stilled as in 4:35–41, and very few of us (praise God) will experience torment like that of the poor 'Gerasene demoniac' (5:1–20). But all of us know about parents' anguish over sick and dying children, and the pain of long-term illness, and social rejection and stigma. The kingdom of God offers shelter to these birds, too, and these stories encourage us to bring our fear, faith and hope to Christ in relation to our version of these very human pains.

6 Faith in action

Mark 5:29–34

Faith is not just a matter of mental conviction, in Mark. Both these stories show how faith and fear go hand in hand, as these two characters push against convention and act, driven by deep need.

The woman pushes through until she is right behind Jesus, and touches his cloak. 'And immediately her flow of blood dried up, and she knew in her body that she had been healed from her scourge' (v. 29, my translation). The use of the word 'scourge' here – as in 3:10 – expresses the thought that her condition was a punishment: and in 3:10 we see too the impulse to touch Jesus, because clearly those with 'impure' conditions somehow knew that, if they touched Jesus, they would not infect him with impurity, but it would work in reverse – he would infect them with his 'cleanness'.

And so it is, here. But the woman is not the only one who senses something in her body. Jesus feels 'power gone out from him' (v. 30). In spite of his disciples' scornful comments (v. 31), Jesus demands to know who 'touched' him – not a random brushing against, but a deeply intended touch of faith. So the woman is not allowed to creep away unseen, but 'fearful and trembling, knowing what had happened to her' (v. 33) she steps forward (this time the crowd parts) and confesses all.

Jairus the synagogue leader would normally spearhead the disapproval over her reckless behaviour, pressing through the crowd. But he is about to confront a huge impurity issue himself: his daughter's dead body. Jesus' words to her dispel all disapproval and offer her back her future: 'Daughter, your faith has saved you. Go in peace, and be healthy from your scourge' (v. 34, literal translation). By using the relational address 'daughter', Jesus restores her to community – and offers her a future of peace and health. Though the emphasis has been on Jesus' power, his words spotlight *her* faith as the agent of her healing: starting with a God-given conviction about Jesus, formulating a daring plan, energising its bold execution – her faith has produced this wonderful result.

For Mark, faith always has this quality: active, daring, venturous, risking all, ready to follow Jesus to death if necessary – and maybe therefore always tinged with the fear this lady felt as she stepped out of hiding that day. What's the quality of the faith you feel?

Guidelines

We haven't yet reached the climax of the sequence of stories we've read this week, which centres on Jesus' challenge to Jairus, 'Do not fear, only believe' (5:36). But we have already seen that *faith*, and its relation to *fear*, is the dominant theme in this section of Mark. On the one hand, faith is the opposite of fear – if the disciples had had more faith, they would not have been afraid of the storm. They would have had the same confidence as Jesus, sleeping trustfully, secure in his Father. Similarly, the demonised man leaves fear behind as he comes into his 'sound mind' (5:15). But on the other hand, faith brings fear with it as we come into close encounters with divine presence and power, like the awestruck disciples in 4:41, and the woman in 5:33. For reflection on this, ask which sort of fear is your closest need at the moment – a fear that you want to lose, or a fear that you want to gain? Or both?

This week's readings show us the kingdom of God in action, and therefore prompt the question, what kind of action does the kingdom demand of us now? Mark sets a little puzzle in 4:35 with his introduction, 'On that day, when evening had come, he said to them, "Let us go across…"': why did Jesus set off *in the evening* to travel across Galilee to the remote, sparsely inhabited south-eastern shore? We must certainly imagine the storm raging in pitch-black night, and Jesus' encounter with the demonised man either while it was still dark or in the very early dawn. Mark tells the story as though Jesus had an urgent appointment with this man, whose reputation must have spread round the lake. Jesus crosses the lake simply to meet him – it is all he does on that far shore, before returning to the much more densely inhabited north-western side.

The kingdom of God reaches out to touch the untouchables, the really lost, those beyond help. What might this mean for the church of Jesus Christ today?

1 Little lamb, arise!

Mark 5:35–43

This story is a great climax to the drama of chapter 5. With Peter, James and John and the girl's parents, we enter the inner room and witness the life-bestowing power of God's kingdom as Jesus gently grasps her hand and whispers in Aramaic *talitha cum* – 'Little lamb, arise!' But with great skill, Mark tells the story in such a way that we, the readers, hear about it through the testimony of her parents, who are told by Jesus *not* to make known what had happened (v. 43). We can imagine what they said afterwards: 'When Jesus came, he said she wasn't dead but only asleep! And when he touched her hand, she woke and got up!'

Was she truly dead? The messenger was sure of it (v. 35), and so were the weeping friends and relatives who mock Jesus for suggesting that 'the child is not dead but sleeping' (vv. 39–40). Presumably the parents were convinced also. But Jesus said not. Most commentators think that Jesus means that, in the kingdom of God, death is no more than sleep. That may be so – but Mark leaves us unsure! Is that really what Jesus means? Or does he express his prophetic awareness that the little girl has not in fact died yet, whatever the mourners think?

The 'messianic secret' – that mysterious veiling of Jesus' identity, the cloaking of his powers – reaches out beyond the text and affects the readers of the Gospel, too. Even though we stand in the room there with Peter, James and John, we still don't know what Jesus did, for sure. It is as if we were actually part of the crowd outside, who simply hear what the little girl's parents say. Why has Mark deliberately presented the story in this way?

Maybe it is because Jairus' decision to believe in Jesus and not to fear (v. 36) *predates* the performance of the miracle. He believes first, not afterwards, like the woman with the bleeding. And the same is true for all of us: finally, faith is a decision to view the world through 'kingdom' eyes, even though the kingdom remains hidden like a seed growing secretly (4:26–27) – and even though there are always other explanations of the things in which faith sees evidence of the kingdom of God (as the inhabitants of Nazareth will agree! – see tomorrow's reading).

2 Unseen, unwanted...

Mark 6:1–6

Yesterday's theme carries on today. This passage rounds off the broad section of the Gospel which began in 3:20: remarkably, we end as we began with people *not* believing in Jesus. In 3:20 onwards, it was his own family. Now we discover that basically his whole home town (Nazareth, see 1:9) agrees with them. In between, the themes of faith and the identity of Jesus have been key, revolving around the question, 'Who then is this?' (4:41). Does he truly speak the word of God (4:1–34), and exercise the power of God (4:35–5:43)?

The people of Nazareth know the answer. They are amazed by his teaching and recognise that he performs 'such works of power' (v. 2), but nonetheless 'take offence at him' (v. 3) – because they already have him sized up, pigeon-holed and written off: 'Is this not the carpenter, the son of Mary and brother of James and Joses and Jude and Simon? And are not his sisters here with us?' The inhabitants of Nazareth *know* him – he's a workman in the village, and his family is just ordinary, like them. Their questions (vv. 2–3) are a good example of the way in which tone of voice carries meaning. These are not surprised, wondering enquiries. Imagine the tone that goes with suspecting a conspiracy – some hidden dirty work – and you'll have it!

No display of wisdom or miracle-working power is going to shift their view. They may even have some pop theology to appeal to – it was quite a widespread belief that, when the Messiah comes, no one will know where he has come from. He will just appear, as if from nowhere. He certainly won't have a job and sisters.

How much do we miss through knowing the answer already? The inhabitants of Nazareth missed out on 'deeds of power': they had heard of them elsewhere (v. 2), but in Nazareth 'he could do no deed of power' (v. 5). The capacity of God's Son to act with kingdom power is restricted by their lack of faith, which thus becomes a self-fulfilling prophecy. The take-away question for us is: do we have fixed viewpoints that close off bigger, more wonderful, unimagined possibilities in the life of faith? There once was an Ugly Duckling... who sadly never looked at his beautiful reflection, and stayed an ugly duckling all his life.

3 Into the deep end

Mark 6:6–13

A new section of Mark's Gospel begins here: 6:6—8:30 begins and ends with a focus on Jesus' disciples, and the theme that runs through this section is their *relationship* with Jesus, their *understanding* of him and their *training* to follow him. The theme appears very challengingly in this passage, with Jesus sending his disciples out in pairs to preach and heal with his authority (v. 7). They are to go with the barest, minimal equipment – with no provision for tomorrow, only for today (vv. 8–9) – and completely dependent on people's hospitality (v. 10). They make themselves defenceless signs of the kingdom, trusting in God's protection and provision, so that when people receive them or reject them, they are receiving or rejecting the message of the kingdom and its power.

If rejected (like Jesus in Nazareth), they are not to fight back, but to 'shake off the dust from the soles of your feet as a testimony to them' (v. 11, my translation). Normally, Jews would do this symbolically on returning to the Holy Land from Gentile territory, so that no Gentile dust would defile Israel. What a powerful symbol, to adopt this action here! Did Jesus do this when he left Nazareth (v. 6)? Places that reject the message of the kingdom are in danger of becoming Gentile – that is, they are putting themselves outside the orbit of the covenant with Israel and its fulfilment in Jesus.

I worked for many years in institutions training people for Christian ministry. Jesus doesn't seem to believe in this! He just sends his disciples out. Training for it *before* doing it could miss the basic point that ministry is not an application of skills, but an exercise of faith. Always! – even though thinking about it is vital, and Jesus seeks to train his disciples' thinking as they spend time 'with him' (3:14).

We should probably not take Jesus' instructions here as the rule for all Christian missionaries. Trouble was caused in the early church by travelling missionaries who used verse 10 as an excuse to outstay their welcome! This mission was a special, symbolic action, ending in 6:30–32. But we can still ask: how can we (more clearly) be symbols of the kingdom of God where we live, expressing publicly its power and reality? What actions would express the reality of the kingdom to those among whom we live?

4 A multitude of opinions

Mark 6:14–16

'King Herod' suddenly makes an entrance – a surprise indeed. Clearly Mark wants to tell the story of the death of John the Baptist (we'll think tomorrow why he wants to do this), but he introduces it with these three verses illustrating the views circulating about Jesus. People are suggesting the amazing theory that Jesus has these 'powers' because he is a resurrected John the Baptist – and even more amazingly, Herod agrees with this: 'John, whom I beheaded, has been raised' (v. 16).

We immediately suspect that guilt may play a role in Herod's explanation of Jesus' powers. But before unpacking this, Mark underlines the variety of views about Jesus. Others think he is Elijah, who was expected as a forerunner of the Messiah (Malachi 4:5–6), and others that Jesus is a new prophet. Luke mentions that some were saying Jesus was a resurrected ancient prophet (Luke 9:8). All of these views are exciting, because it was widely held that prophecy had ceased – there had been no prophets in Israel, like Elijah or any of the others, for several hundred years. Jesus has just referred to himself as a prophet in 6:4.

Into this confusion of opinion the apostles set out. What will they say? The last we heard from them was a puzzled and fearful 'Who *is* this?' (4:41). Do they now know the answer? They certainly do not. (Peter will later have a lightbulb moment – see 8:27–29.) They go out as Jesus' representatives, but they have no clarity to offer to this confusion. Presumably they don't think that he is a *resurrected* John, but they know that there is some connection between John's arrest and the beginning of Jesus' ministry – see Mark 1:14. They have no answers except the powers of the kingdom, working through them in Jesus' name.

This lack of clarity about Jesus' identity is central to Mark's telling of the story. He pulls us, his readers, into the same questioning. Who is this person? What are these powers? And how do we – how do people – find answers to questions like this? One clear aspect of the answer is that those on the 'inside' don't have privileged 'insider' knowledge, so that they know while those 'outside' don't. Is that okay? Could it be okay for the Christian church not to know for sure the answer to the question in Mark 4:41, 'Who then is this?'

5 Holiness and faithfulness

Mark 6:17–20

We are in the middle of a Markan sandwich here. The mission of the twelve begins in 6:7 and ends in 6:30–31, so that the story of John's terrible death at Herod's command is the filling in the sandwich. Matthew makes a time connection between the two – see Matthew 14:12–13 (parallel to Mark 6:29–30). But for Mark the connection is just around the *activity*: this is what happens to the prophetic servants of God who go out with the message 'the kingdom of God is arriving: repent and believe the gospel!' (Mark 1:15). We know from Luke that John was certainly ready to get specific about the changes that people needed to make in their lives (see Luke 3:10–14), and at some point he had been bold and direct with Herod about his marriage to Herodias – with the result described in v. 17.

It's not just that the word provokes opposition. Ultimately, Mark is telling us, God's kingdom runs into direct conflict with all other 'kings' and kingdoms. Autocratic rulers who claim the power of life and death over their subjects – as nations still do, when they send their men and women to war – are actually claiming the authority of God himself, who alone is the giver and taker of life. Rulers are subject to God's rule, whether they like it or not. One of the ironic features of Mark's telling of the story here is that he underlines Herod's lack of power: he listens gladly to John and hears him frequently, respecting his holiness and 'righteousness' (v. 20), but ultimately cannot protect him from Herodias' hatred.

According to Professor Thomas Schirrmacher, about 10 per cent of Christians worldwide (some 200 million people), living in over 50 countries, face danger to their lives because of religious extremism. Persecution of Christians is now more intense than ever, and in many places any attempt to 'preach the word' as here in Mark leads to immediate imprisonment or loss of life. John the Baptist foreshadows all such persecution, and illustrates the enormous need for courage and holiness that we *all* have in today's world. His extended trial before Herod foreshadows the later (much more peremptory) trial of Jesus himself, and illustrates too how the greatest challenge is not to have the right 'answers' but to be able at each moment to live the kingdom life with consistency, faithfulness and freedom from fear.

6 What a waste...?

Mark 6:21–29

It's a famous story which has prompted countless artistic representations over the centuries. What drama! The drunken king manipulated by his cunning wife and her merciless teenage daughter in front of his birthday guests – trying to parade his power but simply displaying his weakness. The story prompts for us a terrible, haunting question: why does God permit his faithful servants to come to such awful ends?

Mark helps us with this question here. But we can gain insight from Revelation, where John pictures the martyrs 'who had been slaughtered for the word of God and for the testimony they had given', crying out, 'Sovereign Lord, holy and true, how long will it be before you judge and avenge our blood on the inhabitants of the earth?' (Revelation 6:9–10). Their question says it all: this God is 'sovereign', so he has the power to arrange the world so that their deaths did not happen. More than that, he is 'holy and true', which means that there is no lack of will to want what is right. So he has both the power and the will first to protect his servants and then to avenge the injustice of their deaths – why does he not do it?

The answer in Revelation is that martyrdom is one of the very special ways in which some bear the image of their saviour. All of us are saved by being joined with him in his death – a union symbolised vividly in baptism – so that we die 'in Christ' when the time comes. Some of us experience that union with Christ in this very direct way, by ourselves dying because of faithfulness to the Lord and 'testimony' to him. In the early church, some Christians actively sought martyrdom, wanting this privilege of dying not just *with* but *for* the Lord. That seems to take it too far – John maintains the 'testimony' of his word until the moment when, beyond his control, it is replaced by the 'testimony' of his death ('witness' and 'martyr' are the same word in Greek).

And what a testimony! – permanently memorialised in this story which foreshadows Jesus' own death at the instigation (in part) of this same Herod – see Luke 23:6–12. John truly is the 'forerunner'. This is Mark's quiet version of the Revelation perspective on martyrdom – John dies just as his Lord will, summarily executed by enemies who reject his word.

Guidelines

Christian theology has struggled throughout the centuries to define exactly who Jesus is. Eventually the church settled on certain forms of words in the creeds, with which as many as possible could be satisfied – but only because the words give maximum room for debate: what exactly do we mean when we say that he is 'the only Son of God, eternally begotten of the Father, God from God, Light from Light, true God from true God, begotten, not made, of one Being with the Father… and was made man'? These words of the Nicene creed are very important, because Christians have been affirming them for nearly 1,700 years – but how amazing, and glorious, that they suggest rather than define, they hint rather than explain, they image rather than realise. So the debate goes on still!

We are in just the same position as the disciples in this week's readings: committed to following, feeling deeply that Jesus is worth following, ready to honour him, keen to part company with those who see no more than a carpenter and a brother – yet not sure who he really is. Praise God for the rest of the New Testament: this is the agenda for Acts and the letters – to dig away at the question, and to explore more fully who this Jesus really is for us, what his death means, how the Holy Spirit of God has now become the Spirit of Christ given to all who trust in him (how amazing), indeed what he is for the whole cosmos, not just for the church.

And yet – again – the New Testament leaves us simply with glorious, powerful words that are like pictures of a reality that cannot be pictured, angle-shots that capture a feature but never the whole, whispers and rumours and tantalising sounds from afar that keep drawing us in, longing to see him more clearly, to know him better.

'Who then is this?' (4:41) Where are you today with this question?

FURTHER READING

Morna Hooker, *The Gospel According to St Mark* (Continuum, 1991).

Open Doors, 'World Watch Report 2017' (**www.opendoorsuk.org/persecution/documents/wwl-report-2017.pdf**).

Thomas Schirrmacher, 'Persecution of Christians today', *Unio Cum Christo* 1:1–2 (2015), pp. 187–207 (**www.uniocc.com/archive/persecution-of-christians-today**).

Tom Wright, *Mark for Everyone* (SPCK, 2001).

2 Timothy, Titus and Philemon

Ian Paul

These three letters, gathered at the end of Paul's writings in our Bibles, are often neglected but offer us some profound insights into Paul's thinking and practice. Alongside Paul's letters to seven churches, it means that (if we include Hebrews as Pauline, which is probably mistaken but was a common assumption in the past), we have in total 14 letters.

2 Timothy and Titus, along with 1 Timothy, are usually labelled the 'pastoral epistles' because they are addressed to pastors who have oversight of some of the early Christian congregations in their area. There has been significant debate about whether they really were written by Paul, in part because some distinct vocabulary is different from Paul's earlier letters, and in part because of what appears to be a different focus on questions of church order, reflected in Paul's concern for the appointment of 'elders'. But, as we shall see, there are many things in these letters which correlate not only with Paul's earlier concerns but also with those of Jesus and other New Testament writers. Compared with the literature that we know from the second century, these letters look thoroughly Pauline.

Philemon is rather different. A personal letter addressed to a friend and fellow leader, it is one of the 'prison epistles' along with Colossians and Ephesians, written by Paul when under house arrest, and never seriously questioned as authentic. Although these three letters are dealing with quite different concerns from his other letters, the portrait of Paul is consistent. In all three, but particularly in 2 Timothy – his last, written knowing that he was near the end of his life – we are offered fascinating insights into his character and thought. Paul, the great theological thinker of the first generation of followers of Jesus and the fearless pioneering missionary and church planter, is revealed as a person of great warmth and tenderness, someone deeply dependent on personal relationships and profoundly hurt by personal betrayal. Together, the letters give us a Pauline combination of passion and wisdom, of victory and suffering, and of both personal and doctrinal insight.

Quotations are from the New International Version (Anglicised).

1 The confidence of faith

2 Timothy 1:1–14

Paul's opening greetings blend together the transformation in his thinking that has come about as a result of his experience of what God has done in Christ, and his tender affection towards Timothy, his 'dear son' in the Lord. And in these opening verses, he holds together important themes in Christian thinking that are often set against one another.

The first pair of themes is the sovereignty of God and the responsibility of human response. Paul is an apostle of Jesus 'by the will of God' (v. 1) and not of his own choosing. In fact, the whole project of our salvation and sanctification is 'because of [God's] own purpose and grace' (v. 9), arising out of God's intention and initiative before time began. Although Jesus' 'appearing' (v. 10) here refers to his incarnation and public ministry, Paul's personal experience on the Damascus road reinforces his sense that God's revelation of himself in Jesus was of his own doing. And yet, for Paul, this elicits not a sense of passivity but of vigorous human response, both for himself and for Timothy. Just as Paul energetically pursued the ministry of being a 'herald', 'apostle' and 'teacher' of the faith (v. 11), so he now encourages Timothy to take action, to 'fan into flame' (v. 6) the gift of God – probably the commission to be a minister of the gospel – to respond with energy to what God has called him to. The Spirit does not take control of us, but leads us into 'self-discipline' (v. 7), to the fullness of human maturity and responsibility. We need to bend our will to 'guard the good deposit' of faith we have been given (v. 14).

This means attending to both the inner life and the outer – to personal discipline and holiness as well as the 'testimony about our Lord or me' (v. 8), meaning either the testimony they offer or the testimony about them. It means experiencing both 'joy' (v. 4) in seeing what God has done in our lives and the lives of others and in the blessing of our new family in the Lord, and 'suffering' (vv. 8, 12) pressure and opposition just as Jesus did. It means looking back with pride ('my ancestors', v. 3) and looking forward in confident hope ('promise of life', v. 1). Paul can put up with public shame because he knows he is honoured by the one whose opinion is all that ultimately matters.

2 Building a people of power

2 Timothy 1:15—2:10

Paul is often characterised as exemplifying 'muscular Christianity', not least because of his tireless activity in preaching and teaching, and his travels around the eastern Mediterranean – he probably walked around 10,000 miles in his ten most active years of ministry. The metaphors at the centre of this passage reinforce this impression. A follower of Jesus is a 'soldier' (2:3, despite the early Christians being uniformly pacifist), engaged in spiritual warfare, not against human forces but against the 'powers of this dark world' (Ephesians 6:12), language that finds its way into many baptism liturgies. Discipleship involves the training regime of an 'athlete' (2:5, though many Jews and Christians saw the Roman games as immoral because of the nudity involved), a metaphor Paul applied to himself as well as others (1 Corinthians 9:27) because he knew that even he had not yet attained maturity (Philippians 3:12–14). And though it is God who sows the seed (Mark 4:3) and who gives the growth (1 Corinthians 3:6), nurturing faith in ourselves and others requires the hard work of a 'farmer' (2:6). These are images that we must return to and reflect on again and again (2:7).

Yet Paul was no individualist. His gratitude to Onesiphorus, who went out of his way to support and encourage Paul (1:16–18), is typical of someone who was keenly aware of his dependence on others – those ahead of him in faith, those from whom he had learnt much and those whose support, ministry and partnership he treasured (Romans 16:1–16). If his words about those who have 'deserted' him (1:15) sound harsh, this reflects the pain of betrayal felt by someone who was a consistent team player. So he urges Timothy to be the same – to build a team of 'reliable' people, whom Timothy can trust and who will share his teaching ministry (2:2). Timothy, like Paul, needs the company of other faithful 'witnesses' who will share his testimony.

This twin focus is rooted in Paul's gospel (2:8), even though the summary here sounds more than succinct. Jesus was fully human, 'descended from David', the anointed king who would fulfil the hopes and longings of his people for freedom and deliverance. And he did this through defeating death as only God could do – through being 'raised from the dead' and ascended to the Father's right hand, sharing his glory and power. This combination of human discipline and divine power come together to forge a renewed 'elect' (2:10), the people of God, both for this age and the age to come.

3 The foundation of faith

2 Timothy 2:11–21

The trustworthy word or saying might be something already known which Paul is quoting, or might be a saying of Paul's. The fourfold assertions, all in the form 'if… then…' align with both Paul's earlier teaching and the teaching of Jesus, and continue the theme of divine and human responsibility.

Firstly, Paul has explained that we 'die with him' as we enter the waters of baptism, and then emerge to new life in anticipation of our final resurrection as we emerge from those same waters (Romans 6:4). This symbolises the reality that, when we are in Christ, 'the new creation has come: the old has gone, the new is here' (2 Corinthians 5:17). Secondly, patient endurance is the hallmark of Christian faith, since we cannot enter the kingdom without going through 'many hardships' (Acts 14:22). But those whom Jesus has purchased and who walk his path of suffering will reign with him (Revelation 5:10). The third assertion echoes Jesus' own teaching in Mark 8:38 (and Luke 9:26) that 'If any is ashamed of me… [I] will be ashamed of them' on the last day. God's gracious offer of new life is free, but it is not cheap, and accepting it requires costly commitment. And yet (fourthly) God always remains faithful, even when we are not, and his offer of forgiveness is always available for those who turn to him.

These are precious truths which God's people need to keep hold of if they are to live this new life in all its fullness. Paul has no time for worthless quarrelling about mere words (vv. 14, 16), whether that is in theological point-scoring or idle gossip. But Paul knows that words matter, and longs that Timothy should handle the words of scripture and of the good news about Jesus like a skilled craftsman who can make a straight cut in a piece of wood (v. 15). This includes the truth about our relationship with God (v. 19) as well as sound teaching or doctrine (v. 18); the two belong together. (The idea of a secret resurrection is not unlike modern teaching about a secret rapture, and is just as misleading.) There is no sense here of spiritual elitism; anyone who commits themselves to live in this truth can be used by God (v. 21).

4 Spiritual leadership

2 Timothy 2:22—3:9

Martin Luther once defined sin as *cor curvum se* – the heart turned in on itself. Here, Paul encourages Timothy to live a disciplined life in order to fulfil his responsibilities as a Christian leader – but it is a life turned, in a disciplined way, not in on itself but outwards towards others. Christian leadership involves being 'kind to everyone', avoiding unnecessary conflict, firmly focusing on good teaching and being winsome to opponents. The point of teaching the truth is not to win arguments, but to win people, so that those who are in error might themselves 'come to their senses' (2:26) and also come to live in the truth. For Paul, it seems, there is always hope, even for those who are 'opponents' of the gospel; even they have the possibility of repentance held out if they 'come to their senses', the phrase Jesus uses of the prodigal son at his turning point in Luke 15:17.

This is a spiritual and not simply a practical or pastoral task – the winning over of others means engaging in spiritual conflict and rescuing them from 'the trap of the devil' (2:26). So 'fleeing the evil desires of youth' (2:22) probably does simply refer to sexual temptation (as is often thought) but includes having the maturity to avoid snap judgements, scoring points over others or getting carried away with power. Timothy needs a wise and steady head on his young shoulders.

This is all the more pertinent because of the character of 'the last days' (3:1). Although there are hints at some intensification of evil towards the end, the 'last days' actually began with Pentecost (Acts 2:17). Paul lists 18 vices in no obvious order, though with some overlap with the list in Romans 1:29–31 – but in striking contrast to the fruit of the Spirit listed in Galatians 5:22–23. The power of true godliness is in the transformation that leads to holy living. This distinctive life is like the difference between Israel and Egypt at the Exodus; 'Jannes' and 'Jambres' are the legendary names of the magicians opposed to Moses and Aaron (Exodus 7:10–12). Just as God's deliverance then became clear, so the difference between true and false godliness will become 'clear to everyone'.

5 Apostolic confidence

2 Timothy 3:10—4:5

This supremely pastoral letter here reaches its climax, as Paul makes his final charge to Timothy before his very personal signing off, setting out three features of apostolic ministry.

The first is that of relationship and fellowship, of shared ministry with others who live that distinctive life and whose teaching he can trust. It is entirely consistent with Paul's ministry throughout the New Testament that he can appeal to Timothy by highlighting the qualities in his own life that have been fashioned after the example of Jesus, just as he did with the Corinthians (1 Corinthians 11:1). But Paul is not unique in this; Timothy also knows the way of life of 'those from whom you have learned' (3:14) the faith, including his family.

The second is that of suffering. Paul still recalls the hard time he had on his first missionary journey in Iconium and Lystra (Acts 14), and repeats here what he said there: 'we must go through many hardships to enter the kingdom of God' (Acts 14:22). His language here echoes Jesus' teaching in the sermon on the mount ('Blessed are you when people insult you', Matthew 5:11) and the theme of suffering forms the centrepiece of Paul's defence of his apostolic ministry in 2 Corinthians 11:21–29.

The third feature is faithfulness to the teaching of the scriptures. Paul treats his scriptures (the Old Testament) as a reliable testimony to the acts of God in and among his people, and he constantly refers to them in communicating the truth about Jesus, the climax and fulfilment of God's action in the world. These now include the New Testament, since the Gospel writers saw themselves as continuing this reliable testimony (Luke 1:1–4; John 20:31–31), and because others soon saw this in Paul's writings too (2 Peter 3:16). These scriptures, breathed out by the Spirit of God, are able to teach what is right and correct what is wrong in understanding, and train right action whilst rebuking wrong action (3:16), just as is the apostolic message which aligns with it (4:2). So Paul urges Timothy to be unstinting in proclaiming the word of God, not just because of the presence of God and Jesus in which they both live, but because of the hope of his appearing (this time referring to his return) at which he will 'judge the living and the dead' (4:1), a phrase now incorporated in the creeds, and when the kingdom at last will be fully present.

6 A life poured out for others

2 Timothy 4:6–22

In this extraordinary ending to his final letter, Paul touches on many of the themes he has already explored, but does so against a brimming sense of confident personal hope. As he has poured himself out for others and for the sake of the gospel in life, so he is now being poured out in death – 'till death Thy endless mercies seal, and make my sacrifice complete' (Charles Wesley, 1707–88). For Paul, death is not the end or a loss, but a 'releasing' into God's future, the literal meaning of the word translated 'departure' (v. 6). He is confident, not just because he has indeed remained faithful to his life's end (compare 2:13) but supremely because of the faithfulness of God who will bring his work to completion in Paul (compare Philippians 1:6).

Once again, Paul is acutely aware of the impact of relationships. There are those who have failed to stay the course and have deserted both Paul and the gospel – Demas (v. 10) and Alexander (v. 14). But just as he has taught others to do (Romans 12:19–20), he does not seek revenge but trusts to God as judge of all. And Paul continues to the end to value those who have worked alongside him, particularly Luke, whose friendship explains the close relationship between Paul's theology in his letters and Luke's in his writings. Perhaps the most poignant mention is that of Mark – the same Mark who bailed out of ministry at an important moment (Acts 13:13), and whose involvement became a serious point of contention between Paul and Barnabas (Acts 15:36–40). Paul not only taught about the ministry of reconciliation (2 Corinthians 5:16–21); he lived it out in his own life.

Paul's concern for reading the scriptures endures to the end – the probable meaning of his request for Timothy to bring 'scrolls and parchments', though this could also include some of his own writings. He ends on a note of continued trust; he knows God has delivered him in the past, and is confident that God will deliver him again – not necessarily from suffering and death at the hands of his enemies, but into the kingdom of God's perfect, heavenly reign. For Timothy, his final wish is for the presence of God to guide him; the grace of God to surround him; and for the glory to be to God in all things. It is a fitting end to a life well lived.

Guidelines

This fascinating final letter contains many striking and challenging ideas. Perhaps one of its most notable features is the way it holds together different aspects of Christian living and thinking which are often either separated or traded off against each other. It is going too far to call Paul's thinking 'dialectic', but the ideas which he holds in tension or relation to one another are things which, on their own and stripped of their counterbalancing partner, easily become heretical.

The first pair is the idea of God's sovereignty and human response. Paul is clear that salvation is not only God's gift, but it is God's initiative from the very beginning. However, this leads him neither to a determinism about who is saved nor complacency about human action. God's initiative calls for – demands, even – human response, not just as an initial reaction but as an ongoing focus. This interaction between the human and the divine finds expression in the person of Jesus, who holds together in himself divine action and human response.

The second pair is the importance of both the personal as well as the corporate. Paul is clear that each person needs to make a personal response to God's invitation, but is equally clear that this then leads to a new corporate identity within the body of Christ. It is presented here in Paul's encouragement of Timothy to personal discipline on the one hand, and Paul's own focus on the importance of relationships with others, something he also wants to see in Timothy. This is a reflection of the way Paul holds together the subjective and the objective; the gospel is about personal experience but it is also about truth; it is about feelings but also about facts. We never find Paul arguing that one of these has priority and the other then tags along.

Lastly, we note Paul's twin focus on understanding and action. He wants people to fully understand what God has done for them in Jesus – but then wants to see their lives changed by this, so that the difference is evident to all.

1 Establishing God's people

Titus 1:1–14

Although Paul follows the usual format of letter-writing here, this one has an unusual introduction, similar only to Romans in its focus. He identifies himself as a 'servant' of God (or Christ) and an apostle or 'special messenger' of Jesus (v. 1); the purpose of servants and of messengers is not to draw attention to themselves, but to serve and point to the one who sent them. But here, Paul expands on his purpose in relation to those to whom he has been sent – to build up God's people in their faith, knowledge of the truth and their hope, and that in turn is to shape godly living. As elsewhere, Paul emphasises that this is not of his choosing, but by the 'command' (v. 3) of God.

This focus is not surprising, given the reason for Paul's writing. Titus is not mentioned in Acts, but is referred to by Paul in his early (Galatians 2:1, 3) and later (2 Corinthians 2:13) writings. He was probably one of Paul's converts ('my true son', v. 4) from a Gentile background, and is not only a trusted partner in gospel ministry (2 Corinthians 8:23) but also someone who can tackle difficult pastoral issues (taking Paul's 'harsh letter' to Corinth, 2 Corinthians 7:12–15) and trustworthy with the collection for the Macedonians (2 Corinthians 8:5–7). It appears that, after Paul's release from the imprisonment at the end of Acts, he and Titus went to Crete and planted churches there, and Paul has left Titus to appoint local leaders. Paul is here not seeking to control what is happening, but to enable the delegation of shared ministry – not correcting problems, as in 1 Timothy, but putting leadership in place to avoid them.

Although Paul only mentions men as elders ('faithful to his wife', v. 6), we know from Romans 16 that he worked with women who shared his apostolic ministry (Romans 16:7). He recognises the importance of living an integrated life – a leader's good standing among believers should reflect his competence as a leader in his own household. 'Hospitality', literally 'the love of strangers', was a notable characteristic of the early Christian community and a concern of all (Romans 12:13; Hebrews 13:2; 1 Peter 4:9). In asking leaders to be 'blameless', Paul is not asking for perfection, but that leaders should be mature in the faith, living distinctive lives in good standing with all, just like the first believers in Jerusalem (Acts 2:47).

2 A healthy distinctiveness

Titus 1:10—2:5

Although Paul is not trying to correct errors that have already crept into churches in Crete, he is aware of the possibilities of danger. Chief amongst these threats are those 'of the circumcision group' (1:10). These seem to be the ones who were arguing that to be a follower of (the Jewish saviour) Jesus, you needed to be circumcised as well – something Paul believed undermined the sufficiency of Jesus' death and resurrection for us, and compromised the offer of salvation to all, both Jew and Gentile. It was a major debate for the early church (Acts 15) and touched on a key part of Paul's understanding of the gospel (Romans 1:16).

Titus had already encountered this debate, since he was in Jerusalem with Paul, and his lack of circumcision was part of Paul's own case (Galatians 2:3). For Paul, Jesus (and he alone) was the 'yes' to all God's promises (2 Corinthians 1:20–22), and nothing needed to be added to the message about him – Paul wanted to ensure that those whom Titus appointed would hold to the same good news. Paul's opposition to 'Jewish myths' (1:14) is not opposition to Jewish faith, or the Jewish roots of Christian faith; he consistently assumes that the Jewish scriptures (the Old Testament) have become the scriptures of all followers of Jesus, Jew and Gentile alike.

Though it sounds harsh, Paul agrees with the Cretan philosopher Epimenides about the failings of his fellow countrymen (1:12) – but that could not describe all the island's inhabitants, else Titus would find no one to appoint to leadership! Paul's concern is rather that Christian leaders are shaped more by the fruit of the Spirit than by their surrounding culture, and that they lead distinctive lives that others should follow. This is quite the opposite to a narrow-minded legalism; the discipline and self-control that comes with mature faith actually allows people to enjoy the freedom that is theirs in Christ ('To the pure, all things are pure', 1:15). Paul here uses a medical metaphor of 'healthy' teaching – translated in most English versions with the rather duller 'sound' (2:1) – a word he uses frequently in the pastorals and not in his other letters, but one which makes a connection with Jesus' own claims to be the one who brings spiritual health (Luke 5:31). Healthy churches need healthy teaching from healthy leaders.

3 Winsome living

Titus 2:6—3:2

It is easy to feel frustrated that some of the ethical instructions in the New Testament don't sound a bit more radical. The apparent acceptance of slavery and the submission to what was in reality a violent autocratic system of government seem too meek and mild and highly conformist – not just in comparison with contemporary Christian ethics, but also compared with the radical ethics of Jesus. It is easy to misread Paul's concerns in two directions – either rejecting them as a failed compromise, or accepting them as a universal agenda for social conformity.

But all letters in the New Testament are 'occasional' – written to people in a particular time and place. The early Christian movement at this stage comprises perhaps 10,000 people in an empire of 14 million, so challenging the structures of the status quo was not an option. And this new way of life was a revelation – but it mustn't look too much like a revolution. Any movement which was seen to be threatening the social order would quickly be put down by the Roman authorities. The message of the gospel was indeed radical, but not in ways we might realise. It offers a radical involvement of all; groups (slaves, women and children) who might be expected simply to do as they are told are appealed to as active moral agents. It offers a radical blessing of all; the ethics here are full of concern for others and kindness to them. And it offers a radical hope – that we will see the full glory of God at the coming of Jesus our saviour (the best way of understanding 2:13). He is the one who not only loves us and accepts us, but effects the radical transformation of holiness in each of our lives.

Paul's consistent concern is that this hope should be made available to all – hence the repeated refrain that opponents should 'have nothing bad to say about us' (2:8) and that 'the teaching about God our saviour [will be] attractive' (v. 10). There were plenty of issues in which the early Christians were distinctive, not least their refusal to worship anyone other than Jesus, and Paul did not want to add any unnecessary barriers. And it worked! Over the next 200 years, this tiny band grew faster than any religious movement in history until it took the empire captive.

4 Oh, what a gift!

Titus 3:3–15

The sharp contrast that Paul has drawn between the moral position of believers and those in wider society could easily give the believers a sense of superiority so that they looked down on others – were it not for two things which Paul now explores.

The first is that he is very clear that believers are, by their own efforts and in their natural state, no different from those around them. It is striking that Paul includes himself, a Jew, in the description of what 'at one time, we too were' (v. 3). The list of seven faults are not just a matter of moral failure, but of being spiritually 'enslaved'; we needed not just teaching but rescuing from bondage. And that rescue has been effected by the one who 'saved' us. The 'washing' alludes to water baptism which acts as a sign of the inner washing by the Holy Spirit. The language of 'rebirth' reminds us of Jesus' teaching in John 3, that we must be 'born again', but the particular term Paul uses hints at the new creation, the new world that God's anointed one brings into being. When we are born anew of water and the Spirit, we begin to live the life of the age to come – the meaning of 'eternal life' (v. 7).

But the second thing Paul emphasises is that the change we have experienced is all God's doing – it is his 'mercy' and not our merit by which we have received this gift. In Paul's day, gift-giving was governed by strict protocols; you gave a gift to a person who merited it by their worth, and the greater their worth, the greater the gift you gave. But God turned that system upside-down in Jesus; the greatest gift of all has been given to those of no worth at all, but by the sheer kindness and generosity of the giver.

Having received this gift, however, is only the beginning. In the light of God's generosity to us, we now seek to be generous to others by 'doing what is good' (v. 8). There is no point in Titus engaging in 'foolish controversies' (v. 9) that will not change anything; focusing on responding to God and sharing good news in word and deed will avoid the pitfall of living 'unproductive lives' (v. 14).

5 Transforming relationships

Philemon 1–11

It is perhaps surprising to find one of Paul's personal letters in the canon of the New Testament, especially as it does not appear to be concerned with obvious issues of ministry, leadership or doctrine. But it is significant in giving us an insight into how Paul handled a difficult situation.

The first part of this short letter is dominated by Paul's establishing of his strong relationship with Philemon before he turns to make his personal request. Luther called this letter 'holy flattery', and some have suspected Paul of being manipulative and underhand – but in fact the kinds of things he focuses on here are present in his other letters. He deploys the language of friendship and family (Apphia 'our sister' in verse 2 might well have been Philemon's wife) which he uses frequently elsewhere; having been born of the same heavenly Father, all those who believe are now members of one family which transcends natural family ties. He also emphasises shared commitment and ministry; Philemon is a 'fellow worker' (v. 1), a term Paul uses for those who shared his apostolic ministry, who seems to be the leader of the Christian community ('church' is too institutional a term for *ekklesia*) meeting in his home. Another member of his family (perhaps his son?) is addressed as a 'fellow soldier'; the imagery of fighting as a soldier is one that Paul and others use elsewhere (1 Corinthians 9:7; 2 Corinthians 10:3; Ephesians 6:10–13; 2 Timothy 2:3; 1 Peter 2:11).

But the theological basis of their relationship is matched by one of personal experience. Paul prays for Philemon, his family and his fellow believers, and 'always' (v. 4) gives thanks for them, as he does for many others (1 Thessalonians 1:2; Philippians 1:3; 1 Corinthians 1:4). It is typical that Paul's concern in verse 5 is both upward ('faith in the Lord Jesus') and outward ('love for all his people'), and that he sees discipleship not simply as having a decisive beginning but as also involving a continuing journey of 'deepening understanding' (v. 6). And, also typically, Paul is reluctant to demand anything even when he would be entitled to do so; instead, he prefers to 'appeal to you on the basis of love' (v. 9). The quality of relationships within the body of Christ are no mere abstraction for Paul, but make a practical difference in the way that he relates to his brothers and sisters.

6 The practice of reconciliation

Philemon 12–25

In past debates among Christians about slavery, both sides have appealed to this letter. On the one hand, Paul appears to take the institution of slavery for granted, and offers no obvious objection to it. After all, up to one third of the population of the empire were enslaved, and an ending of the institution would have brought the social and economic structure crashing down. And yet the language Paul uses here challenges the very assumptions that make slavery possible.

It appears as though Philemon's slave Onesimus (whose name means 'useful') has run away ('separated from you', v. 15), possibly because he stole some money ('if he... owes you anything' v. 18). He has met Paul, either by seeking him out or in his imprisonment, and has become a Christian through him ('my son', v. 10). Paul's affection for Onesimus ('my very heart', v. 12) outstrips even the warmth of his greeting to Philemon – but instead of seeking the freedom of the slave, or allowing him to go his own way, he seeks reconciliation between the two which will transform their relationship. The language of verse 16 ('no longer as a slave') is rather ambiguous; Paul does not appear to be suggesting that Philemon should grant Onesimus manumission – setting him free – but does assume that the fraternal relationship between fellow believers will both transcend and transform the social relationship that already exists.

This reconciliation involves at least three things for Paul. Firstly, it means Paul making costly decisions to prioritise the reconciled relationship over his own needs and preferences. He would rather have kept Onesimus with him, as a support in his confined situation, than send him away. But his commitment to Philemon means doing what is right by him. Secondly, it means Paul 'standing in the gap' and being ready to bear the cost of whatever it will take to restore the relationship and right what has gone wrong. Thirdly, Paul is committed to maintaining his relationship with both parties as they come together with one another. Not only does he emphasise his continuing partnership with Philemon (v. 17), he also commits to coming to him again in person (v. 22). For Paul, the reconciliation effected between us and God through the death and resurrection of Jesus (2 Corinthians 5:18–19) was not simply an useful idea or a handy metaphor – it was something that shaped his own life and relationships.

Guidelines

These two letters of Paul, with their attention to two very different issues, have less of a sense of urgency about them, and less personal disclosure than many of his other letters. However, they are marked by Paul's continued concern for truth in teaching and truth in relationships.

Having entrusted to Titus the task of leadership among believers in Crete, he hopes that Titus will in turn find people he can trust and who are trusted already. It is no surprise, then, that his focus is on character rather than gifting, and on people for whom the transformative impact of the good news is evident. But Paul is also concerned about the truth of the doctrine that they receive, so that they can pass on to others what Paul himself received and passed on, first to Titus and (through him) to these others. The distinctive nature of Christian belief, and the way that it sets apart its followers from their surrounding culture, means that it is all the more important to have no stumbling blocks to faith; leaders must present no unnecessary obstacle that would distract from holding out the offer of life which they themselves have received. The renewing life of the age to come must be lived out persuasively among those still living in this age which is passing away.

Christian truth will only be persuasive when it is lived out in practice. Paul's exposition elsewhere of the reconciling power of the good news is expressed in his own concern for reconciliation between Philemon and Onesimus, when both might have good reason to choose another path. Paul is committed to rebuilding relationships, even at cost to himself – and the preservation of his personal letter is most likely testimony to the fact that what he longed for did in fact happen. Paul's concerns here have continued relevance to us. How can we make sure we (and those around us) are rooted in healthy teaching, and how can that be expressed in healthy and health-giving relationships? How can we communicate God's offer of reconciliation – and how can we live it out in an ever-divided world?

FURTHER READING

John Barclay, *Paul and the Subversive Power of Grace* (Grove Books Ltd, 2016).

Gordon Fee, *1 and 2 Timothy, Titus* (New International Biblical Commentary) (Hendrickson, 1984).

Ben Witherington, *The Letters to Philemon, the Colossians and the Ephesians* (Eerdmans, 2007).

Tom Wright, *Paul for Everyone: The pastoral letters* (SPCK, 2003).

Leviticus

Henry Wansbrough OSB

The book of Leviticus, the third book of the Bible, forms part of the law of Moses, the Pentateuch. Traditionally, therefore, it draws its authority from Moses. This does not by any means imply that from a literary point of view it stems from Moses. In fact, it is largely a guide to the rituals of the second, post-exilic temple. Some of the regulations date from the post-exilic period, perhaps in the fifth century BC. Others originate from 1,000 years earlier or more, dating from the time when Abraham and his clan were nomadic shepherds.

What value, then, has this collection of ancient laws for Christians of the 21st century? It enshrines a conception of God, particularly the awesome holiness of God and the spirit in which his servants should approach him. This holiness must be reflected in that of all who come into contact with God, the whole people of God, but especially in those who function as priests. Contact with defilement – and defilement comes from anything which smacks of death or decay – must be purged and cleansed by God's own life-giving force.

At the same time, constant and careful respect is shown for human needs, and any behaviour which takes advantage of fellow human beings or limits human freedom, especially the poor and the weak, is outlawed.

In the second week, we continue to reflect on the curious ancient code of law and ritual which has so much to teach us through the principles on which it is founded. With refreshing directness, the Bible has no hesitation in speaking about that very sacred and intimate subject: sex and its purpose, the amazing privilege of the creation of life. Nor does it shun laying down principles for that other basic human instinct: revenge. This teaching causes difficulties for Christians who attempt to follow the teaching of Jesus on forgiveness, and forces us to reflect on the progress of revelation, how God gradually nudges us to a fuller understanding of the divine nature and our obligations as made in the image of God. We also reflect on the holiness of God, what this means and how we can show our sorrow for our neglect of the divine sanctity. Much of this is reflected in the liturgy prescribed for festival days, Atonement, Passover and Jubilee.

We begin the meditations for the first week with a consideration of different kinds of sacrifice and of the investiture of priests, going on to some forms of defilement. It is worth stressing that these comments are personal reflections rather than definitive claims.

Quotations are from the New Revised Standard Version.

1 Sacrifice: holocaust

Leviticus 1:1–10

Sacrifice of the produce of the land was an essential part of the expression of Israel's relationship with God, but there were several kinds and several different purposes of sacrifice. Historically, one clear distinction is between animal sacrifice and the offerings of grain and wheat products. The former (as we shall see in reflecting on the Passover) goes back to the days when the Hebrews were nomadic herders; the latter begins in Israel only when they were settled agriculturalists. In the former, blood plays an important part, which does not seem to have been an important part in either Mesopotamian or Egyptian religion. It is, however, important in ancient Canaanite practices. When the Hebrews/Israelites entered Canaan (more or less the area of modern Israel and Palestine), they seem to have adopted many of the religious practices of the previous inhabitants, applying them no longer to Baal but now to their own God.

The basic form of sacrifice is called 'holocaust'. The name comes from the Greek 'wholly burnt'; the Hebrew word *ola* is related to 'going up' – it goes up in smoke. The point of the holocaust is that the beast or grain offered is totally destroyed. That is, it is given over to God as a recognition that everything comes from God and that we owe to God everything that we have. It is therefore a pure thanksgiving. The offerer places his hands on the head of the beast not, as in some other rituals, as a sign of transference of sin, but as a gesture indicating 'This is mine that I give to the Lord, part of myself'. The offering must be pure and unblemished, not soiled by sin or imperfection.

Blood is particularly important, as a sign of the life given by God. I once witnessed (in a foreign abattoir) the slaughter of a great, fertile, snorting, champing bull. A shot into the head from a humane-killer felled it, but then the throat was cut and warm blood flowed out in unbelievable torrents. What remained was just an inert hunk of meat. There was no doubt that the life was in the blood. The recognition that life belongs to God and comes from God alone is expressed in the use of the blood. In some rituals, it is daubed on the altar and sprinkled on the people as a sign of life and a gift of life. It can cover up faults and revivify what has been soiled. Far from being negative and 'creepy', in Hebrew ritual blood is a wholly positive agent, close to God and bringing close to God what is touched by blood.

2 Sacrifice: communion sacrifice

Leviticus 3:1–5

This is the most common form of sacrifice. The Hebrew name *shelamim* is derived from the word *shalom*, the word still commonly used as a greeting in modern Hebrew, and meaning 'peace' or 'well-being'. The symbolism shows that the beast is shared between offerer and God – with the priest also getting a look-in. At first sight, one might think that God is given the nasty and dirty bits! In fact, to God are given the life-giving parts (kidney, liver, generative organs and fatty parts – we can live off our fat) as a recognition, once more, that life comes from God. God does not, of course, consume these parts, but this is presumably the symbolic meaning of their being burnt on the altar.

However, the description given here is of the formalised offering in the temple. Informally, and before the founding of the temple, the situation was simpler. In the earlier situation, it looks as though *shelamim* was simply the name of a good meal with meat (an indulgence, as it still is for most of the world's population) shared with the Lord, such as at the proclamation of Saul as king (1 Samuel 9:24) or the celebration of David bringing the ark up to Jerusalem (2 Samuel 6:17). At Shiloh, the priest had no special portion as in the present legislation, but took 'pot-luck', simply sticking his fork into the pot and taking for his own whatever the fork skewered (1 Samuel 2:13). It looks as though on these occasions the 'well-being' was shared between the members of the community as much as between them and God.

The situation must have changed radically at the reform of King Josiah, some 20 years before the end of the Israelite monarchy. In an attempt to eradicate pagan practices and fertility rites which had crept in, Josiah centralised all worship in Jerusalem (2 Kings 23). How effective was this legislation? It is essential to remember that the rules laid down in Leviticus are somewhat theoretical, designed for the post-exilic community, a much smaller group, huddled round Jerusalem, and within easy reach of the temple. They may have little relevance to the practice and worship as lived before the Babylonian exile.

3 Sacrifice: atonement

Leviticus 5:15–20

With its plethora of prohibitions and regulations intended to express and safeguard the sanctity of God, the law was bound to include adequate machinery for repairing damage to the covenant relationship, especially because uncleanness could often and easily be incurred automatically and without any moral guilt or even unawares. Such uncleanness is the more important if it involves the high priest or the king, since they are representative of the community. The chief feature of these sacrifices is that, though the important and generative parts of the beast offered are burnt in the usual way, the remainder of the flesh is not eaten, but is simply carried away and burnt (4:13).

For Christians, the most striking aspect of these sacrifices for atonement is that no repentance seems to be involved. Defilement is incurred by the disturbance of the proper order of things, and is expunged by a sacrifice which is deemed to restore it. Contrition, being sorry for sin, plays no part: there is simply an automatic repayment. A fully developed ritual, either religious or social, always brings with it the danger that the ritual may be seen as an end in itself, rather than as expressing religious or human values. This is more intensely the case when atonement is seen as simply restoring the correct order ordained by the Creator.

This does certainly not mean that Israel had no consciousness of sin, but simply that sin was in a different register, and had no part in the sacrificial system of atonement. From the earliest prophets, there is constant complaint against sacrifice without justice and without repentance:

I hate, I despise your festivals, and I take no delight in your solemn assemblies. Even though you offer me your burnt offerings and grain offerings, I will not accept them... But let justice roll down like waters, and righteousness like an ever-flowing stream.

AMOS 5:21–22, 24

When Israel's repeated rebellions forced the Lord to send them into exile, the consciousness of sin became more and more vivid, and indeed dominated the spirituality of the chosen people from then onwards. It almost seems that there is nothing but laments and self-accusations, especially in the Psalms, many of which are post-exilic: 'Wash me thoroughly from my iniquity and cleanse me from my sin... for my sin is ever before me' (Psalm 51:2–3). The same psalm continues, 'You have no delight in sacrifice... the sacrifice acceptable to God is a broken and contrite heart' (v. 16–17).

4 Priestly ordination

Leviticus 8:1–3; 9:22–24

In this matter, above all it is important to distinguish history and theory. The presentation of priestly ordination of the sons of Aaron is a historical fiction; the temple priesthood cannot be traced back to Aaron. Worship of the Lord in the temple of Jerusalem cannot have begun till the temple was built by Solomon. Before that, there is only occasional mention of priests at various shrines round the country, e.g. Ahimelech at Nob (1 Samuel 21:2). Worship was centred in Jerusalem by the abolition of other shrines only shortly before the exile by King Josiah. After the exile, the temple priests attributed their priestly lineage to Zadok, who may have been a Jebusite priest of Jerusalem rather than an Israelite, perhaps taken on by David with the Jebusite liturgy of Jerusalem when he captured the city and made it his capital. The description of the commissioning of the priests given in Leviticus is dependent on the ordination of the high priest, an office which came into being only at the return to Jerusalem of the exiles from Babylon.

The chief lesson to be learned from the ceremony is the awesome holiness of the priests: the ceremony is intended to show how they share in the holiness of the God whom they serve. The book of Leviticus is all about holiness, and one of the chief ways in which the holiness of God is shown is the special position of the priests who share in and reflect that holiness in a special way. Hence there are two principal parts to the ceremony: the sacrifice of atonement for their sins, to remove obstacles to their participation in divine holiness; and the anointing with blood, the symbol of life which belongs to God, which always signifies reinvigoration with divine life. This gives them the ability to act as intermediaries between God and the people.

There is a sharp distinction between these priests and priests in the Christian church. There is no mention in the New Testament of any men or women who function as Christian priests. There is only Christ, the high priest, in whose priesthood the whole Christian people share: 'He loved us and has washed away our sins in his blood and made us a line of kings, priests to serve his God and Father' (Revelation 1:5, JB). The principal teaching of the letter to the Hebrews is that the high-priesthood of Christ is of an altogether different order to that of the Aaronite priests, the order of Melchizedek (see Hebrews 7).

5 Clean and unclean food

Leviticus 11:1–8

The rules given in Leviticus for clean and unclean food are far from easy to explain. One popular explanation is hygiene: pork is forbidden because in desert conditions (no fridges!) it so quickly becomes inedible. Shellfish, too, are notorious causes of stomach upset; the only fish which may be eaten are those which can be salted. Scavengers such as vultures are forbidden because of the dangers of contact with corrupt and decaying flesh. Non-leaping insects may be forbidden for the same reason (11:20–21), contracting uncleanness by dragging along the ground. Regardless, insects can hardly provide much of a meal, though some types of locusts, which are permitted, can be as big as shrimps; laced with wild honey, they seem to have sufficed for John the Baptist (Matthew 3:4).

While these factors may have played their part, there were others, too. Idolatry played its part in the prohibitions; it may be that pigs were forbidden food because they were plentifully used in sacrifices to the gods of Mesopotamia, Abraham's land of origin. The current strict Jewish prohibition of consuming meat and milk together (not in the same dish, not at the same meal, not with the same utensils, not in the same fridge) is part of the 'fence round the law' to insure against any possibility of slipping into the Canaanite practice of boiling a goat-kid in its mother's milk, which was supposed to have some magical powers.

However, the list given in this section can leave the innocent reader totally bewildered. One of the principles is consistency. The Hebrews seem to have had an idea of fixed species and wholeness, and a corresponding horror of mixtures. So one ideal is provided by the ox and cow, ruminants with cloven hoof; then beasts which lack one or other of the characteristics of the ideal are unsatisfactory, as though not purebred. It is as though God created a tidy world of fixed species and boundaries which should not be crossed – no genetically modified crops for them! It was even forbidden to have clothes made out of two different fibres (19:19), or an ox and a donkey under the same yoke for ploughing. It was a matter of homage to the Creator: God created a stable world, and human beings should respect the world as God made it, not mixing things up. Every creature had its specific function, and observance of this was part of recognition of the Lord's sovereignty.

6 Leprosy

Leviticus 13:1–6

Leprosy in the Bible is a very different thing from the modern definition. It affects not only human beings but also buildings and fabrics. The common factors seem to be decay and infection. This becomes clear in the following chapters which deal with the testing of 'leprosy' in fabrics and buildings, with the aim of establishing whether it is still spreading or is already 'dead' and therefore no longer contagious. The severity with which it is treated in non-human situations suggests that the horror comes from other factors than merely a patch of damp (14:37–38), even to the extent of pulling the whole house down if the 'leprosy' persists (14:45). This may be connected with the idea of God's creation: he made all things and repeatedly 'he saw that it was good'. The antithesis of this is decay, directly contrary to God's creative designs. There is a strange little ceremony of purification in 14:4–7 involving two birds: the one bird is killed to obtain its blood, the other is smeared with the blood, and so reinvigorated with God's gift of life, and then allowed to fly off into the open country. Might this suggest a primitive belief that the disease is brought by a winged demon?

Even in human beings, too, the classification is far wider than modern terminology would allow, covering many other skin diseases than what is now commonly (and more precisely) known as 'Hansen's syndrome'. The biblical expression includes many forms of skin diseases, especially infectious ones. Contrary to popular belief, Hansen discovered in 1873 that 'Hansen's syndrome' itself is not highly infectious.

The rules for leprosy in human beings are centred on isolation to prevent the spread of contagion – an isolation which may well have been more harrowing than the ravages of the disease itself: the ten lepers in Luke had to 'stand afar off' (Luke 17:12). The stories of Jesus' approach to lepers are supreme examples of his carefree love for those in need. Transcending all the rules of health and safety, he has no hesitation in touching the leper (Mark 1:40–42). It is notable that Jesus is not rejecting the law as such, for he still tells the cured leper to observe the Mosaic regulations. It is just that, for Jesus, love and sympathy for the sufferer come higher up the scale of values.

Guidelines

Leviticus dedicates some time to talking about leprosy. My one visit to a leper colony, at Mutemwa in Zimbabwe, was harrowing in the extreme. Many of the sufferers had progressed much further in the disease than was inevitable because, in consequence of the shame of the disease, they had been kept hidden when they could have been treated at an early stage. Consequently, they had lost movement and feeling in their extremities. They were a courageous group of people, and delighted to meet a visitor, despite their gnarled and cramped limbs. They were benefiting – too late – from modern medical care, but it gave a quite new meaning to the sympathy and love shown by the Son of God to the distorted and isolated sufferers whom he met. When we visit the sick, we cannot normally cure the disease, but the expression of care and sympathy lends the sick person strength and encouragement.

Reflect on your own experience of meeting sick people and those with terminal illness. How did you express God's love to them? Make a list of people you know now in these conditions and commit to pray for them once a day.

1 Sexual uncleanness

Leviticus 15:1–5, 19–24

'Uncleanness' is, from our point of view, the wrong term. Sex is sacred and, like all the processes of life and death, must be treated as special. In the same way, the holy scrolls are said to 'soil the hands': those who touch them must wash before and afterwards, to indicate that the scrolls are set apart from ordinary life. It is in this way that sex, too, is set apart – not unclean but eminently sacred. In the same way, touching the dead brings 'defilement'; that is, the dead must be treated with reverence, for the hand of God has been laid upon them and they have entered into the mystery of God. To the believer, the dead body is no mere corpse, but ineradicably carries an aura of reverence and awe.

The mysterious beginning of life, too, deserves the same wonder and respect, not only from the awesome intimacy of man and woman, but from the intimacy of the couple and their act with God. Made in the image of God as we are, we are called to complete his creation by peopling the world, and in no other act is our imaging of God so awesomely reflected. No matter how far scientific analysis may detail it, we cannot understand the beginning of a new life. When a woman is said to be 'unclean' for a certain time after giving birth (12:1–8), this is a further assertion of the sacredness of the moment of birth.

There are other aspects, too. The loss of blood at certain moments may play its part, for blood is the sacred symbol of life, and loss of blood indicates diminution of life, which must be given time to be restored. More relevant to us today is the element of the protection of women: her 'uncleanness' means that she is to be free at sensitive and vulnerable moments, such as the postnatal time, from male sexual attentions. Further restrictions (18:1–30) are to protect the family: the 'forbidden degrees' provide a defence against inbreeding, important in a closed society. (The invention of the bicycle was a crucial factor in opening up the gene pool from one village to another!) Furthermore, there is a different sort of intimacy between members of a family where sexual attraction and sexual intimacy play no part: a different sort of love.

2 The Day of Atonement

Leviticus 16:3–10, 17–20

Yom Kippur, or the Day of Atonement, is perhaps the most important religious day in the calendar for modern Jews. In the days of the post-exilic temple, there was an important ritual of reconciliation, though many scholars hold that it is never mentioned in pre-exilic texts. Consciousness of sin is one of the features of post-exilic spirituality.

The temple ritual consisted of two parts, one negative, one positive. The negative part was a strange archaic rite, somewhat superstitious: the high priest symbolically placed the sins of all Israel on the head of a black goat, which was then driven out into the desert, the haunt of death and demons, where it – and the sins – disappeared. This was called the goat 'for Azazel', Azazel being presumably the name of an evil spirit domiciled in the desert. The positive part was a cleansing or re-enlivening of the 'mercy-seat' and of the altar of sacrifice. The 'mercy-seat' or *kapporet* was the cover of the ark, the very place where God was thought of as residing among his people, and where, in the tent of meeting and later in the temple, God could be approached. These two objects were sprinkled with blood, for blood is an especially sacred symbol of life. It belongs to God alone and may never be consumed. It may, however, be used as a cleansing, that is, a re-enlivening agent. The agent and symbol of life in animals and humans was seen as renewing the effectiveness of these sacred objects.

This ritual has a precious echo in the New Testament, for Paul in Romans 3:25 calls Jesus the *hilasterion*, 'mercy-seat' or atonement, 'whom God put forward as an atonement by his blood, effective through faith'. Jesus Christ is the mercy-seat in whom God and humanity are brought together.

For modern Jews, as there is no longer a temple for this rite there is another, very meaningful ritual, which Christians may well bear in mind and even learn from. On the eve of Yom Kippur, everyone asks pardon of family, friends and neighbours (it can be done by telephone too!): 'I am sorry I parked my car across your drive, that my dog ate your cat, that our noisy party went on so late, that I snapped at your mother, that I left you to do the dishes.' Teacher apologises to students as well as students to teacher. As a black cloud drifts off to the horizon, a great air of peace, harmony and friendship reigns. Christians could well learn from this.

3 The holiness code

Leviticus 19:1–4

Leviticus 19:1—20:26 is bracketed by the declaration, 'Be holy for I, the Lord your God, am holy.' It is the heart of the so-called 'holiness code' (chs 17—26) which is especially formed to underline the holiness of God. God's holiness is repeatedly cited as the model for human holiness.

I well remember an occasion when I and two young friends got lost in the Judean desert (through my bad compass-reading), and after walking for four hours were near exhaustion through lack of water. Suddenly, on the sabbath too, a jeep appeared from nowhere and picked us up. Probably saved our lives. As we bumped along, 'wadi-bashing', he called it, there followed a fierce argument with the Israeli driver about the purpose of the law: was it primarily social, to regulate the conduct of God's people, or more specifically to express and safeguard the holiness of God? Where is the focus, God or humanity?

But what is God's holiness? An otherness, yes, but in what sense is God wholly 'other'? No human being, even Moses on Mount Sinai, could see God and live (Exodus 33:20). Elijah covered his face before coming out of his cave to encounter God (1 Kings 19:13). The very name of God, 'the Lord' (YHWH), is too holy to be pronounced. The book of Isaiah is marked from beginning to end by the divine title, 'the Holy One of Israel', whose vision in the temple both drew and daunted the prophet (Isaiah 6). The reaction can only be terror: 'Get among the rocks, hide in the dust at the sight of the terror of the Lord, at the brilliance of his majesty, when he arises to make the earth quake' (Isaiah 2:10, JB). St Augustine speaks of the *mysterium fascinans et tremendum*: an awesome mystery which fascinates and attracts but causes terror. God has an unrivalled attractive power, but don't get too close! And yet YHWH is a God of tenderness and compassion, rich in kindness and faithfulness, as we find echoed in countless passages throughout the Bible.

The theme of the holiness code is that God is faithful, but not to be trifled with; to be approached with confidence, but with a loving respect which outweighs any other human emotion. To enable us to understand a little better, God sent us the Son, the symbol, image, sacrament of God, to express the godhead in all its aspects.

4 The Festival of Passover and Unleavened Bread

Leviticus 23:5–14

For Christians, the most important Jewish festival is that of Passover and Unleavened Bread. Jesus made this festival his own by adopting it for the celebration of the new covenant, the acted prophetic prequel, so to speak, of his sacrifice of himself to the Father. It is now celebrated in the Eucharist, the central act of Christian worship. Of this, the centre is the Lamb of God and the unleavened bread.

The two elements of the festival have wholly different origins, and it is by chance that they come together. The Passover was originally a nomads' festival, marking the move from winter pastures in the lowlands to summer pastures in the cooler uplands, celebrated (by moon-worshippers) at the first full moon of spring after the spring equinox (now 21 March). Its centre was the offering to the goddess of a prime lamb or goat-kid as a thanksgiving, and to turn away any wrath of the deity. As always in Israelite sacrifice, the blood smeared on the doorposts is a symbol of life. This nomadic rite, at the beginning of the trek to the uplands, was no doubt practised long before the exodus from Egypt, for Abraham, Isaac and Jacob were nomads too. It was adopted as the rite to celebrate the beginning of the great trek of 40 years on the desert at the deliverance from Egypt. It is more fully described in Exodus 12.

The Festival of Unleavened Bread is an agricultural festival, and cannot have begun before Israel settled in Canaan and began ploughing and harvesting grain. It celebrates the beginning of the grain harvest, the first sheaf of barley. The bread is unleavened because all the produce of the previous harvest is thrown out and new yeast has not yet had time to ferment.

The two elements are the more easily combined because they occur at roughly the same time of year, and both include unleavened bread. Nomads do not remain stationary long enough to ferment yeast.

5 Retaliation

Leviticus 24:17–22

What should Christians, governed by Jesus' teaching on forgiveness (seventy times seven) and turning the other cheek, make of these laws? Most Christians nowadays find the death penalty repugnant, and yet here it is automatic for killing another human being. We can look at the law of retaliation in two ways.

On the one hand 'an eye for an eye' was a notable advance. It is not a specifically biblical teaching, but – like many of the social laws of the Bible – occurs in all the law-codes of the ancient Near East, notably the Code of Hammurabi and the Code of Eshnunna. Its function was not to prescribe revenge but to limit it: *only* an eye for an eye, not a greater revenge. You can't kill someone who puts out your eye! Historically also, this biblical legislation is impressive for its egalitarianism, giving all human life the same value. Many of the Near Eastern law-codes lay down different penalties for offences to different classes of people, so that offences to noblemen, commoners, slaves and foreigners incur different classes of penalty. In the biblical legislation, they are all equal – a fundamental bill of human rights!

But the difficulty of 'tit-for-tat' remains: did God change his mind between the Old Testament and the New? Is it really true that the God of the Old Testament is a God of wrath, whereas the God of the New Testament is a God of love? No one who has digested the definition of the divine name, YHWH, given to Moses can countenance that: 'A God merciful and gracious, slow to anger and abounding in steadfast love' (Exodus 34:6).

However, here enters in the fundamental idea of gradual revelation. It took Christians a long time to realise the implications of the teaching of Jesus. Despite all the biblical teaching to the contrary, as long as physical strength dominated social relationships, we regarded women (the 'weaker sex') as somehow an inferior species. For centuries, we tolerated the idea of slavery of Christians to Christians. Even Paul (in his letter to Philemon) does not push the truth that we are all brothers and sisters in Christ to the logical consequence of abolishing slavery. For many centuries, we thought that an agonising death for those who held a different interpretation of Christian belief would please God – the martyrs of the Reformation witness to that. It seems that the Lord teaches us only what we can gradually come to understand.

6 The jubilee year

Leviticus 25:8–17

Seven is the sacred number. Why? The most stable and visible timing-factor of all of the heavens is the moon, with its cycle of 28 days, or four times seven. (It took a long time for the exact length of the solar year to be calculated!) The ancestors of Abraham may well have worshipped the moon, which is why the Hebrew day begins in the evening, at moonrise – not like the tidy modern day which begins at midnight. Other traces of the sacred number remain, such as the division of the first creation story into seven days, with God resting on the seventh.

So on the seventh (sabbath), day of the week, everyone rests, and in the seventh (sabbatical) year, even the land rests. But after the seventh week of years, that is, 49 years, comes the great jubilee, announced by the *yobel* or trumpet. Whether the sabbatical year or the jubilee year were ever observed is another matter, but it is the principle that matters. It was asking a lot to refrain from exploiting the land in the seventh year, but to refrain from working the land also in the following year, the year following the seventh seventh year – so two consecutive years – was a really tough demand.

Like so much of the biblical legislation, this legislation has two dimensions, divine and human. The most important principle of the legislation is that all land belongs to the Lord, and the earthly 'owner' is no more than a temporary tenant with the right of making use of the land and its harvests: 'you are only strangers and guests' (Leviticus 25:23, JB). So every seventh year (every sabbatical year) the land enjoys the same rest as the Creator himself – there is no ploughing or planting or any cultivation – and every jubilee year the land reverts to the Lord, and secondarily to the original owner. So if land is 'sold', what is in fact sold is the produce for the number of years remaining until the next jubilee. This legislation is therefore a sort of protective social blueprint for stability. The owner of ancestral property is never left wholly destitute, but can always rely on the Lord for the eventual return of the land, making a fresh start possible.

Later in the chapter (25:35–41) comes similar legislation about slavery. Although a Hebrew may own Gentile slaves, a Hebrew can only be 'a hired man or a guest, and shall work with you until the jubilee year' and may not be harshly treated. The Hebrew hired man (and his family) retain their fundamental human dignity, and revert to full freedom at the jubilee year.

Guidelines

Beneath its surface meaning of instructions about the temple liturgy, and such dated matters as blood rituals, ritual cleanliness and land holdings, the book of Leviticus has lessons to teach us. We learn about the nature of God, or at any rate how we should approach his holy presence, for no human being can see God and live. We learn something also about our treatment of human beings, the honour and respect due to all men and women, and how that can be expressed in various aspects of our lives. Perhaps above all, we learn the unfailing care and love of God for the whole of creation. These were the principles by which, in a bygone age, the people of the post-exilic temple expressed their devotion and prepared for the coming of Christ.

Zephaniah and Habakkuk

Brian Howell

Zephaniah wrote during the reign of King Josiah, 640–609BC, whereas Habakkuk wrote roughly in the last part of the seventh century, when the neo-Babylonian Empire was on the rise. By this time, the last faithful king, Josiah, had been killed at Megiddo, opposing Pharaoh Neco II on his way to the Battle of Carchemish (605BC). Neco was in turn defeated by the neo-Babylonians, led by Nebuchadnezzar II in a world-changing battle like Trafalgar or Waterloo. The king of Judah, Jehoiakim (608–598BC), initially submitted to Nebuchadnezzar as a vassal, but later rebelled, incurring the first of two deportations that would spell the end of the kingdom of Judah. Both Zephaniah and Habakkuk include the sorts of judgements from God typically associated with prophets and, yet, each extend light for hope.

Zephaniah is a little-known prophet appearing in 2 Kings, Jeremiah and Zechariah. The 'Day of Yahweh' is the major theme of his series of oracles, discussed in several aspects, and its dating is closely linked with Josiah's reform. His book is a literary masterpiece, interweaving themes of judgement and pride, humility and shame, morning and night with great artistry and purpose.

Habakkuk also lived at the nadir of the southern kingdom, during Jehoiakim's reign. We don't know much about the prophet himself, as, unlike other prophetic books, we don't have information on his lineage or hometown. The extra-biblical addition to Daniel, 'Bel and the Dragon', contains a supernatural incident where Habakkuk is flown by an angel to give his lunch to Daniel while he was in the lion's den. However, both early Jewish and later commentators adopt a rather negative view of the prophet. The French philosopher Voltaire once said, 'That rogue is capable of anything,' and joked that he 'smelt too strongly of brimstone' to be tolerated by pious Protestants (Thomas Heath, *Faith Amid the Ruins: The book of Habakkuk*, Lexham, 2016, pp. 1, 27). Why would this be? In Habakkuk, we find a man deeply conflicted about the suffering and sin of his people, and his response to God can, to some, seem unseemly, even rebellious. But Habakkuk is no Jonah. He doesn't run away from God's message of judgement, but presses into it, showing us a way to grow in our faith by boldly putting the tough questions of life back to the God who raised them.

Unless otherwise stated, quotations are from the New American Standard Bible.

1 *Dies irae*

Zephaniah 1:1–3

Zephaniah is unusual among Old Testament prophets in that he was not actually called a 'prophet,' or *nabi*, in the professional sense (cf. Isaiah 1:1; Habakkuk 1:1). Even the fig tree grower and shepherd Amos was a *hozeh*, or 'seer', but Zephaniah gets no such title. In fact, we don't know much about him. His mini-genealogy of four generations is more substantial than that of other prophets whose singular reference serves simply as a surname. Though there is some debate, it seems that Zephaniah was related to King Hezekiah, grandfather of the current king (Josiah). Though one generation younger than Josiah, Zephaniah is not one to pull his punches, and is thought to have had some influence in Josiah's reform.

The main theme is undoubtedly 'the Day of the Lord', a day of judgement, and yet whose object, purposes and results are less than straightforward. The book is structured by seven sets of speeches (1:2–7; 1:8–17; 1:18—2:6; 2:7–11; 2:12—3:5; 3:6–13; 3:14–20), which alternate between God and the prophet speaking, as seen in the shifts between first and third person.

The first oracle explodes out of the gate with a reversal of the entire created order. All the creatures are destroyed in reverse order of their creation, but humanity's demise is emphasised again as they have been deposed from their dominion over the earth. The darkness mentioned signifies the creation has returned to its primordial, chaotic state (cf. Zephaniah 1:15; Genesis 1:2). This devastation, however, serves more as theological statement than promised action. If this had literally been carried out, the subsequent threats would have been rendered meaningless. The reference both to creation and flood (de-creation) presents this prophet's message in a uniquely universal framework. Rather than simply the internal issues of covenant adherence, the prophecy concerns all the inhabitants of the earth. However, as it was addressed to Judahites, and probably never made it before pagan kings, this universalism is in service of a greater message. In one sense, it is the Creator demonstrating his power over creation, saying, 'I brought you into this world... I'll take you out!' In another, it is a direct rebuke of the Judahites' proclivity to adopt the mores and worship practices of other nations, as the destiny of these are also clearly under the control of Yahweh.

2 Spiritual dimensions

Zephaniah 1:4–11

The Day of Yahweh not only has political fallout, but also a spiritual dimension. Indeed, the first reasons given for the judgement are the worship practices of Judah and Jerusalem. The condemnation of the priests demonstrates how far these spiritual leaders had fallen in breaking the second of the ten commandments. Some are adjured for turning their fealty towards created objects – the stars. Others simply opt for syncretism, attempting to practise both faiths.

All of these culminate with 'those who have turned back from following or enquiring of the Lord' (v. 6). 'Following' involves responding to God in all arenas of life: his commands on how to conduct oneself with others (morality), and instructions on how he is to be approached (worship). 'Enquiring of God', however, adds another dimension – discerning the future in order to act appropriately (wisdom), as well as requesting needs of sustenance, fertility, justice and security. Those who have turned from following and enquiring of God seek power to live from outside the relationship with their Creator.

In verses 7–9, God mocks the worship of those people who do not really follow him. Now, he prepares a sacrifice, as a grand feast, only to expose those who are not really true to him. They come wearing foreign clothes rather than their prescribed priestly attire, making exaggerated displays of 'worship' within the temple, but perpetuating the sort of violence dishonouring to Yahweh.

Not only are these first among the specific targets of God's wrath, later we find a threat made directly against foreign deities. In 2:11, we find Yahweh promising to 'starve the gods'. This is not an image of spiritualised conflict in the heavens, as much as the practical effects Yahweh will produce to eradicate false worship. Idols were typically seen by their worshippers as alive, and, as such, were not only adorned with jewellery and fine clothes, but continually offered feasts of food and wine. In fact, the ancient Near Eastern creation tale *Enuma Elish* depicted humans as being created solely for the 'feeding' of the gods. Similarly, after the flood in the *Atrahasis* myth, the gods were 'starving' and flocked like flies to the sacrifice offered by the Babylonian counterpart to Noah. To 'starve' the gods thus entailed the cessation of the worship rites that brought them food, whether by the extermination of the cult itself or their worshippers. Either way, the gods themselves lose their influence.

3 Judgement

Zephaniah 1:12, 2:4–15

Yahweh's wrath is triggered by the attitudes taken towards him (1:12) and targets a surprisingly wide geographical area (2:4–15). Judah considers him weak and turns to other gods (1:4–9). The nations see Judah as weak, and assume her god is as well (2:10). Assyria boasts it is supreme and there 'is no other' (2:15). Such maligning of God's power, both by those who should know him and those who don't, is found intolerable by their Creator (see *Zephaniah: A prophetic drama*, p. 78).

Notably, those who are indifferent will be judged alongside those who commit acts as treasonous to Yahweh as idolatry (1:12). S.R. Driver speaks of those Zephaniah calls 'stagnant in spirit':

The figure is taken from wine, which, after the process of fermentation was complete, was left upon its sediment or 'lees'... only long enough to fix its colour and body. If not then drawn off, it grew thick and syrupy – sweeter indeed than the strained wine, and to the taste of some more pleasant, but feeble and ready to decay.

Driver, *The Minor Prophets*, p. 118

Though seemingly innocuous in not standing against Yahweh, these present a more insidious alternative than even that of other religions. Far from being inoffensive, their 'pragmatism' is actually a thinly veiled assault on the reality of Yahweh. If he is only a deistic god – one who sets the world in motion and leaves it to its own devices – then he is not the God the Bible describes as having compassion on all that he has made, and a deep-seated interest in fulfilling the potential with which he infused it.

The scope and depth of the judgement is profound. Not only will the covenant people be judged, but her close relatives to the east (Ammon and Moab), mortal enemies from the west (Philistia), major powers to south and north (Egypt and Assyria) and even distant nations (Ethiopia). This last mention is brief and odd, but Calvin seems to think that if a nation that is far away is not to be forgiven, then how much less Judah's neighbours. I would add: how much less Judah herself!

God continues around the compass, until he hits all its points, his message being that he rules over all nations, holding them to account. This is also true at all levels of society. Not only will the syncretistic priests receive the brunt of Yahweh's displeasure, but those who rule, business owners, warriors and peasants.

4 Back to Jerusalem

Zephaniah 3:1–10

As we begin chapter 3, the subject turns from the nations back to Jerusalem. There is some implied comparison between Nineveh and Jerusalem in that both receive the designation 'city', but Judah comes out looking even worse; it is Judah who is called the 'tyrannical' one, not the war-mongering and brutal empire of Assyria. Though every aspect of her society is condemned, from the judicial to the religious, the economic to the military, it is the spiritual aspect that again surfaces as the primary cause of judgement – Judah did not call upon or draw near to her God. It is the lack of a relationship with God which leads to the following abuses of power.

Comparing 2:1, 5, 9 with the present chapter, John D.W. Watts notes:

The people of God are usually called a 'people' and the word 'nation' is used mainly for the heathen… but here, Jerusalem is deliberately classed with the foreign nations, as it will be again in 3:1–7. It has become so foreign in its ways that it seemed to belong more to them than to God.

Watts, *The Books of Joel, Obadiah, Jonah, Nahum, Habakkuk and Zephaniah*, p. 164

Another conundrum in this passage is the reference to Yahweh 'within her' (v. 5). This is parallel to Judah's princes who are 'lions' (v. 3) within her, which implies that they both inhabited the city simultaneously. If this is the case, how was Yahweh's justice expressed within her when all of the people who represented him in terms of the courts, the temple, the military and business were so corrupt? Notably, much of the corruption is pictured taking place at night. In verse 3, the judges are as wolves at evening, leaving nothing for the morning, whereas God brings justice every morning. In the Hebrew, 'in the morning' is repeated twice, before 'God will bring his justice' and it is followed by 'and he [it] will not fail' (v. 5). Both of these phrases strongly underscore the regularity of God's justice – as dependable as the sun coming up tomorrow. This would seem to indicate that God exposes the corruption of those who are to represent him in positions of power. This would also explain the contrast in the last part of verse 5 – the unjust know no shame. Though their deeds done in darkness are brought to light, they continue to commit their injustices, as it were, to God's face.

5 The remnant

Zephaniah 3:11–13

The theme of the remnant initially surfaces in 2:7, 9, foreshadowing 3:11–13. This is full of irony, in that the very nations who are punished for taking Judah's land after she is being humbled by other nations (Philistia, Moab and Ammon) are the ones whose land will become Judah's inheritance and plunder. But even before this, in 1:4, we have seen that Baal's remnant will be destroyed, whereas those who follow Yahweh will inherit the land of their oppressors.

However, we also find that this remnant isn't simply the 'lucky few'. Rather, they are the ones who humble themselves before Yahweh (2:2–3). It is notable that it is only a possible reprieve – 'perhaps you may be hidden' (2:3). This forces those who would humble themselves to truly throw themselves upon God's mercy, rather than using the 'humbling' as yet another source of prideful entitlement. This response, rather than demonstrating their righteousness, also serves to distinguish the remnant from the prideful within Judah (1:4–13) and the nations.

The same element that made the conflict is its resolution – the Day of Yahweh. The removal of the sinful people is necessary to allow the humble to thrive. The solution is God's, not people's.

Verse 11 contrasts subtly with 3:5 in how it treats shame. Whereas the unjust knew no shame, here it is the city itself which would no longer be, or feel, ashamed. Ironically, when the arrogant, unshame-able people are removed from the city, the shame that the city feels as a whole is taken away. Not only this, but they are now distinguished from the nations, who were indicted for their pride as well (2:8, 15).

In contrast with the wicked of Judah who do not bother to call upon God (1:6), but fill the temple with violence and deceit (1:9), the remnant are characterised by their trust in God (3:12), and their lack of deceit (3:13). In humbling themselves before God, the remnant essentially become what Israel should have been.

It is in this that, as Paul House says, 'Hope springs out of judgement' (*Zephaniah: A prophetic drama*, p. 70). As horrific and potentially destructive as they are, even forest fires are purifying, and even deemed necessary from time to time, as they clean out the dead wood that was choking the growth. Similarly, when the wicked and unjust are removed, despite the residual effects and collateral damage, what is left is finally able to grow again.

6 From shame to fame

Zephaniah 3:14–20

Suddenly, we find a call to rejoice (v. 14). Why this celebration? In verse 15, the king, Yahweh, is in the midst of Jerusalem and has taken away her judgement. This seems a bit odd, as we haven't heard that he had left. Rather, he was simply ignored. His justice brought no sense of shame; no one sought his counsel or his ways. This scene is described in the past tense, as a *fait accompli*, as though God has already erased Jerusalem's judgements, and taken away her fears. But in verse 17, we find this is still to come. This is the prophet's way of saying that as sure as the judgements will come, so the day on the far side is inevitable as well.

In verse 17 we find a new thing – Yahweh, the great warrior, joins in singing with his people. No longer the dispenser of judgement, God surprisingly finds great joy in his people – a new people who humble themselves, seeking and honouring him. But his joy is not only in them. We also find the nations reinvited to join God's kingdom so they too might call upon the Lord, and serve him 'shoulder to shoulder,' which probably includes the remnant itself (3:9). In fact, the purpose of the oracles against the nations was to purify the nations' lips so they too can call on him properly (*Zephaniah: A prophetic drama*, p. 78). Furthermore, the now purified nations have an ongoing role as witnesses to what God has done for his remnant.

The restoration in chapter 3 echoes the judgement in chapter 1 with many predictive statements ('I will...') on behalf of Yahweh. The scope too, is worldwide, just as the judgement was. But it is not merely physical. God focuses on the shame which caused some to grieve over the festivals – either because they could not celebrate them during the period of judgement, or, more likely, because of the mockery the prideful Judeans had made of them. This shame, along with that of the abuse hurled at the humble remnant, the dispersed, the lame and the oppressed, will be turned into, literally, a 'name' (vv. 19–20; 'renown', ESV). God will not only restore fortunes, but he will create something new out of the tragedy – thus redeeming the seemingly wasted days of shame and judgement. He builds honour for those who humble themselves before him, and thereby for himself as the one who brings honour from shame.

Guidelines

With life's pressures constantly in our faces, it is all too easy to forget the size of our God. Neither the localised deity of primitive Hebrew superstitions, nor the creation of Western philosophical constructs, the God of the Bible is bigger than our church, tradition or even our nation. Our fate is thus linked to that of other people. In what way might our own sin have negatively impacted the unbelieving community around us? What ongoing role might God have for those currently unbelieving neighbours, faiths or cultures around us beyond judgement of their current ways? Will we pray and act in light of these?

One of the sobering thoughts we are confronted with in Zephaniah is the nature of our worship. Jesus' parable in Matthew 22:1–14 describes a king calling his subjects to his wedding feast, but being rejected for mundane interests. He then calls all, both evil and good, but rejects the one who comes without wedding attire. Similarly, it is not our own goodness that makes us right with God, but how we receive his invitation. Will we give him honour by how we 'clothe' ourselves, either with wedding attire to celebrate him or 'foreign' garments which disregard him or honour others? What behaviours and attitudes do these attires represent in your life?

Sometimes apathy feels neutral, but it can be far more insidious than atheism. While the latter says, 'it isn't true', the former says, 'it doesn't matter'. Indifference thus renders our faith irrelevant by ring-fencing its purchase on our lives and relationships. It implies that Yahweh won't act, so he doesn't matter. If this is so, then something else must matter more – whether the idols who 'will react' to our worship, or simply our own human strivings and cleverness which will 'get results'.

Where have we found room in our tragedies for new growth? In what areas do we find ourselves living out of a pride of comparing ourselves to others – whether favourably or not? In what ways might this hinder growth in others, or ourselves?

Finally, Zephaniah challenges our reaction to the status quo. Is there anything we truly 'grieve' over within our churches, or our nations, or do we assume 'that's just the way it is' and mould our faith accordingly? Have we been those leaders who, grown overly familiar with the politics and procedures, straplines and strategies of the church, end up 'winging it', and thereby missing what Yahweh sought all along: a people humbled before him, who seek him as indispensable?

FURTHER READING

Ehud Ben Zvi, *A Historical-Critical Study of the Book of Zephaniah* (Walter de Gruyter, 1991).

S.R. Driver, *The Minor Prophets Nahum, Habakkuk, Zephaniah, Haggai, Zechariah, Malachi* (T.C. and E. Jack, 1906).

Paul R. House, *Zephaniah: A prophetic drama*, JSOT 69 (Almond, 1988).

Johannes Vlaardingerbroek, *Zephaniah* (Peeters, 1999).

John D.W. Watts, *The Books of Joel, Obadiah, Jonah, Nahum, Habakkuk and Zephaniah* (Cambridge University Press, 1975).

1 First complaint

Habakkuk 1:1–4

Habakkuk's name is the subject of much debate, and is either related to an Akkadian word for a particular 'plant' or to an embrace or hug that keeps one warm and secure. The latter may either reflect his ability to stay rooted, or God's embrace which preserves through judgement (Kent, *Have Faith Anyway*, ch. 1).

Habakkuk's initial lament addresses the problems of the Judean society. One of the things Habakkuk complains about is that the law is ignored (v. 4). During the reign of Josiah, the 'book of the law' was rediscovered after a cleaning out and restoring of the temple which had fallen into disuse during his father's reign. Many scholars see this as the book of Deuteronomy.

The prophet finds grounds for his appeal in God's self-commitment to Israel, seen in the use of his covenant name Yahweh, rather than a pure philosophical assertion of divine duty. Furthermore, there is a well-acknowledged parallel between Habakkuk's complaint and that of the enslaved Israelites in Egypt. In Exodus 2:23–25, we find God responding to his covenanted people precisely by hearing their cries and delivering them. Here, however, the same cries that were formerly heeded now seem to have fallen on deaf ears.

His cry of 'violence!' is the term *hamas*, and is used for many things, from the violence the world had descended into before the flood (Genesis 6:11, 13) to that of a malicious and false witness in court (Deuteronomy 19:16), and is often connected with plots to defraud the poor, vulnerable and upright in society (Micah 2:6; Malachi 6:2). Hence, the sense is not merely that people are going around beating each other physically, but that they are constantly scheming and defrauding one another. Thus, framing the innocent for crimes or legislating away help for the poor is seen on a par with literally stabbing them in the back. The result of this is that, as Roberts observes:

Because God did not uphold the sanctions of the law, the credibility of the law's demands had been undermined, and thus justice never emerged... because God allows the wicked person... to 'hedge in'... the just or righteous person... the only justice that emerges is a perverted, crooked justice.

Roberts, *Nahum, Habakkuk, and Zephaniah*, p. 90

2 First response

Habakkuk 1:5–11

Though there is no formal transition, verse 5 represents the shift from Habakkuk's complaint to God's response. Oddly, however, he addresses not just the prophet, but the whole Judean community. Thus, both in terms of form and content, the shock value is intended.

God responds by saying that he will deal with the wickedness in Judah, but will do so by raising up Babylon ('the Chaldeans', v. 6) to exact the punishment. This, in some sense, would be like God saying he would use a group like ISIS to punish the church. Babylon was not only a kingdom bent on controlling the entire Near East and beyond, but also one who did so brutally, and in service of other gods.

The main question has to do with where the shock value lies. As Roberts observes, the use of the Babylonians as a rod of punishment would hardly come as a surprise after their victory at Carchemish, and concludes that this oracle ought to be dated after Josiah's reign ended in 609, and before the Babylonian ascension as a dominant world power in 605. However, this assumption of surprise contradicts the reputation that the Chaldeans are said to: have a swift and organised military (v. 8), be proficient at siege warfare (v. 10) and have a history of acquiring new lands (v. 6). This might not have been so clear prior to their victory at Carchemish, just as they were not seen as a threat a century earlier in Hezekiah's day (Isaiah 38—39).

Part of why this was a shock was that Hezekiah had befriended the emissaries of the Chaldean king, Merodach Baladan, when they were just trying to break free from Assyrian domination. King Josiah had even lost his life intervening against the Egyptians on behalf of the Babylonians. Hence, it may have been more astonishing that this former ally had turned on Judah. Rather than the newness of the Chaldeans' ascendancy to world power, it is God's abandoning his people to this new power that leaves them speechless.

However, there is a hint of the impermanency of this coming situation. Verse 7 speaks of the justice and authority of the Chaldeans 'originating from themselves'. And yet, one verse earlier, we find God as appointing them to this task. This indicates a great disconnect between the real and perceived sources of authority. God reaffirms the truth of the situation – the one who makes a god out of his own strength will be put to shame (v. 11).

3 Second complaint

Habakkuk 1:12—2:1

In Habakkuk 1:13, God's eyes are said to be too pure to look on evil or wickedness. Surely, though, this doesn't mean he cannot engage with it, as if it were his kryptonite. To understand this, we must look into what 'looking on' entails. It is not a mere scanning of the room to see what's there, as if God wouldn't know about evil unless he physically witnessed it in action. Rather, it has to do with a sort of look of approval or confirmation. Consequently, it isn't that God cannot look at people who are sinning, and is thus blind to the world around him, but that he cannot condone, and thus bless and bring to fruition, what is done in rebellion against him.

Some commentators have postulated that Habakkuk may have had a priestly background (as did Ezekiel). In 2:1, the prophet states he will 'stand at [his] post, and station [him]self on the rampart, and [he] will watch to see what [God] will say to [him]'; terms like 'post' and 'rampart' can refer to the temple, and enquiring of God, and watching and waiting upon his response are activities common for priests. Added to this are traditions from texts like 'Bel and the Dragon', which paint Habakkuk as a Levite (Thomas, *Faith Amid the Ruins*, p. 31). If this is so, we find Habakkuk's complaint part intercession, part prophecy.

The prophet's question of whether or not God should allow such a nation to 'swallow up' those more righteous than they is a double-edged sword (1:13). Perhaps God is implying that the Judeans aren't any more righteous.

The prophet complains again here that the Babylonians sacrifice to their nets and hooks, because through these things their catch was good. On the surface, it would very much seem the Babylonians' power was in their technology and military, or fishing, prowess.

However, it is notable that all the images used for the Babylonians – thieves, raiders, and an unjust builder – evince a transient, fleeting sort of power. The Babylonians might think of themselves as secure and in control, able to punish whom they will, but this is illusory. This hope is confirmed in the statement, 'We will not die' (v. 12). Babylon only has power because God appointed them. Because he is the source of power, his precious ones are still safe, at least from annihilation, if not punishment.

4 Second response

Habakkuk 2:2–20

Habakkuk 2:4 famously speaks of faith through comparison of the haughty with the righteous (cf. Romans 1:17; Galatians 3:11; Hebrews 10:38). Though the old Greek versions tend to see the proud as the Babylonians, the Hebrew texts point to the unfaithful Israelites.

The righteous are to live, and survive, by their faith. The word translated 'faith' is *emunah*, which indicates fidelity or steadfastness. It builds on verse 3, which presents the vision as one coming in its due time, but one which thus requires an active seeking of God – a waiting upon him. The Israelites could live through the coming judgement, by staying the course and trusting God, despite the circumstances. Like Habakkuk himself, they could take a stand like watchmen on the wall (2:1), seeking not the enemy, but signs of the Lord making good on his promise.

This faith, though, requires hope for a different future, even if one cannot see how that may come about from present circumstances. This is where God gives Habakkuk an answer to his concern about the godless Babylonians having free, unfettered reign over his people.

Amidst the many points listed where Babylon will get its due for terrorising the nations, a striking statement occurs. In verse 14, the purpose of the heavenly king is laid out. In contrast with the rulers of Babylon, who seek simply to make themselves secure at any cost (v. 9), God is determined to make his own glory known not just to Israel, but to the nations. For this reason, he will bring Babylon to justice – so that all will realise that no nation or ruler has ultimate authority, but instead will answer to the one who does.

This explains the reference to the futility of idol-making and worship (vv. 18–20). The key here is not only that the idol has no breath in it, but that it is manmade. It is merely a reflection of what the kings or worshippers desire. This is presented in stark relief against the living God who is in his 'holy temple'. Though this could refer to the physical temple, as yet still standing, as the vision looks past the invasion and destruction of Jerusalem, this most likely refers to his heavenly abode. Whereas there was no spirit (also translated 'breath') within the idol, the true spirit of God, the true authority still reigns and is not manipulated by men.

5 Prayer

Habakkuk 3:1–15

According to Thomas (in *Faith Amid the Ruins*), we see a progression in the prophet's own personal development. In his initial complaint, we find him bewildered by the injustice that God allows to continue. But God's response – to use a godless nation to punish his own – only confuses him further. It is not until we find ourselves in chapter 3 that we see a change in the prophet. This change is one that is almost a signature of the psalms, the move from lament, or complaint, to praise. What can we make of this move?

It draws our attention to what changed the prophet (or psalmist). What happened that made them drop their complaint and give glory to God? Sometimes it involves a physical intervention that demonstrates God's attention and care for the writer. Other times, this *volte face* is precipitated through a new perspective given, such as in Psalm 73 due to his vision of the final end of his current enemies. These catalysts often came in the form of prophetic oracles. For Habakkuk, this must have been his vision not only of the impending doom, but of coming out the other side. God would neither let evil triumph, nor the righteous be forgotten. His use of the wicked to punish his own does not constitute an endorsement.

But, why have the complaint in the first place? Why not just praise, all the time? The complaint itself has several functions. Firstly, it reflects genuineness in the writer's approach to God. A lament wrestles with the tension between the real and the ideal. The prophet/psalmist will not feign thanks for things that do not honour God, nor will they sugarcoat the situation to make God look good. Secondly, lament represents a healthy response to that which is not good in life. Our desires to give people their due may occasionally be on target, but rarely will they result in any positive change in others. Instead of revenge or taking things into his own hands, Habakkuk takes them to the only one who can bring about not only justice, but repentance and transformed lives.

Finally, the lament sets the stage for God's intervention. With either a veneer of false praise or problems with only simple human fixes, human life does not make room for a real God. A lament says, 'Things are not as they should be, but only God can make it right.' This effectively puts the ball in God's court, which then allows, and even depends upon, God to intervene. This results in an unfabricated praise which is undeniable and irrepressible.

6 Prophet's response

Habakkuk 3:16–19

In Habakkuk 3:16–19, we find one of the most recognisable lines in the book. How will he face the coming destruction? It most certainly is not through rose-coloured lenses. The vision still terrifies him and the very thought of it makes him sick (v. 16). His is no whitewashed sense of optimism. He mentions the lack of produce, both animal and fruit, though it will not be a famine that is to beset his nation, but a conqueror. However, this too will result in a lack of productivity, as the land will be devastated, the people taken away and any fruit or livestock reappropriated by their enemies.

What is Habakkuk's final answer to this coming doom?

He answers with the metaphor of the deer, though, unlike Psalm 40, it has nothing to do with thirsting for God. Rather, he quotes King David's own expression of praise after a victory (2 Samuel 22:34). This speaks of how God has given him feet like the hind, able to climb high upon the mountains without falling. Interestingly, mountain goats are able to climb amazingly steep cliffsides, both to safety as well as to find food when danger is near, or the more easily attainable food has gone.

But the poet is saying more than this. God being his strength and giving him feet that find secure footing where others cannot results in God 'making [him] walk on [his] high places' (v. 19). 'High places' refers not only to the mountaintops, but was also the technical term for places of worship which were found there. They were condemned by prophets after Jerusalem was established as the only valid sanctuary site, but this was because syncretistic or pagan worship was then driven there. Before the inauguration of the temple, high places were also used for Yahwistic worship, and apparently with no censure (1 Samuel 9:12–25; 10:5, 13; 1 Kings 3:2–4). Here, the prophet may be asserting that God will help him find places to connect with him, even after Jerusalem is sacked and the temple profaned and destroyed. In this way, the prophet points not only to a hope beyond the judgement and coming destruction, but to a new sort of relationship to be had with Yahweh, beyond the temple-oriented cult.

Guidelines

Habakkuk begins with a complaint. But his is not of the same ilk as our own usual mutterings and rants. It is based upon God's covenant with his people. It starts with what God has committed himself to do rather than simply what we want him to do. This gives his argument more teeth, as often our own whims, and sometimes even deepest dreams and passions, may not lead to what is best for us, not to mention others. Do we evaluate our situations upon our own comfort or satisfaction? What legal or spiritual basis do we employ when bringing our complaints against God? The answer is often none, but not always. In those cases, are we, like Habakkuk, bold enough in our relationship with God to call him to account for what he has promised to do?

In Habakkuk, we find that God can use anyone – even those like the Babylonians, whom we might deem furthest from him. This raises several questions: have we dismissed people, or turned a deaf ear to them, because we thought they were unusable by God? What is the last time you can recall hearing God's voice – his wisdom, his confirmation, his rebuke – through those outside the faith? Do we remain open to this as we take our stand in a posture of active, watchful, waiting upon God?

In scripture, it is not always the 'heroes' with whom we are intended to identify. How might we actually be behaving as the Babylonians, assuming that because God has used us to reprove someone else, or implement his will, that we are then above reproach? God uses us for tasks, but this is no rubber stamp of divine approval on all that we do. How many church leaders have we known who have been both used by God, and later 'fallen' due to their own hubris? Are we acting in the same way?

Finally, what can we learn about the nature of faith from Habakkuk? Are we real with God about the injustice we feel? Do we sugarcoat our lives before presenting them to God, or will we lay them bare, in all their awkwardness, seeming contradictions and confusion? What props up our faith? Does our own walk with God consist solely of the devotional insights, obedient service and passionate worship of others? In which areas of our life do we need to ask for hind's feet rather than different terrain?

FURTHER READING (HABAKKUK)

Keith Kent, *Have Faith Anyway: The vision of Habakkuk for our times* (Jossey-Bass, 2008).

J.J.M. Roberts, *Nahum, Habbakuk, and Zephaniah* (John Knox, 1991).

Heath A. Thomas, *Faith Amid the Ruins: The book of Habakkuk* (Lexham, 2016).

The fruit of the Spirit

Ian Macnair

The ninefold fruit of the Spirit listed in Galatians 5:22–23 is not a pick-and-mix stall but a unified picture of Christian character. At the head of the list is love and it can be argued that it encapsulates all the others. In Paul's list of virtues in Colossians 3:12–14, he writes, 'Put on love, which binds them all together in perfect unity.' Joy, forbearance, kindness, faithfulness and self-control are all said to be characteristics of love itself in 1 Corinthians 13.

However, we are not trees or bushes; our lives cannot be fully defined by the categories of horticulture or agriculture. In 1 Timothy 6:11, Paul writes, 'Pursue righteousness, godliness, faith, love, endurance and gentleness.' *Pursue* love.

Fruit indicates God's part in the development of our Christian character and behaviour, and only God can do that by his Holy Spirit. Pursuit indicates our part and God will not do that for us.

Love is not only commended in the Bible; it is commanded. Love is practical, involving actions. It is not based on feelings, but on obedience to Christ's command. It involves loving the unlovely and the unloveable. It *is* the fruit of the Spirit: only God can create this kind of love in us. At the same time, it must be our pursuit, an act of obedience, our love for the Lord in response to his love for us.

In the first week's notes, we will explore in some depth aspects of love and in the following weeks engage with the other constituent qualities more rapidly.

Unless otherwise stated, quotations are from the New International Version (Anglicised).

1 Some aspects of fruitfulness

John 15:1–16

Fruitfulness is a recurring concept from Genesis to Revelation. God's first command to human beings was, 'Be fruitful and increase in number' (Genesis 1:28), possibly the most popular of all God's commands. The Psalter begins by describing the person who is 'like a tree planted by streams of water, which yields its fruit in season' (Psalm 1:3). The very last chapter of Revelation speaks of 'the tree of life, bearing twelve crops of fruit, yielding its fruit every month' (Revelation 22:2).

Fruit has to be attached to the source of its life in order to grow. In Matthew 7:16, Jesus said, 'Do people pick grapes from thorn-bushes?' Grapes don't grow unless they're attached to the vine. In the same way, we have to be attached to Christ by faith. In John 15:5, Jesus indicates that only a living, vital relationship with him guarantees fruitfulness in our lives: 'Apart from me you can do nothing.'

The fruit of the Spirit described in Galatians 5 is nothing less than the life of Jesus in us – the things we see in Jesus: his love, joy, peace, patience, kindness, goodness, faithfulness, gentleness and self-control. We can't live that way in our own resources. We need his life flowing to and through us.

Fruit doesn't mature overnight; it takes time. In Jesus, we do see the fruit of the Spirit in all its fullness, all its perfection, but it takes time to grow in us, which is why some Christians seem unloving, unjoyful, lacking in peace, patience, kindness, and so on.

The very fact that the Lord waits for those qualities to develop in our lives is itself a strong demonstration of his love for us. If Jesus demonstrates his patience, his kindness, with us in this way, we need to view our fellow Christians in the same way.

Fruit is for the benefit of others. The fruit of God's Spirit in us is intended for the good of other people: showing love, spreading joy, making peace, and so on. Fruit is a harvest for the benefit of others, to enhance their lives. It is true that this focus on others does benefit us, but paradoxically it does so by making us less self-centred and diverting our attention away from ourselves.

2 No greater love

Romans 8:28–39

'Greater love has no one than this: to lay down one's life for one's friends' (John 15:13). This comes in the context of Jesus' last words to his disciples before the momentous events of Gethsemane and Good Friday. Jesus himself was to lay down his life for his friends.

In John 15:9, we see the pattern of love: 'As the Father has loved me, so have I loved you.'

There's a striking promise to the faithful remnant among God's Old Testament people in Malachi 3:17: 'I will spare them, just as a father has compassion and spares his son who serves him.'

Compare that promise with another great New Testament passage on love, Romans 8: 'He who did not spare his own Son, but gave him up for us all' (v. 32). How does that tie in with the logic of the Malachi promise? Was God not a God of compassion? Was Jesus not God's son? Was Jesus not supremely the servant of the Lord? Should God not have spared him, just as a father has compassion and spares his son who serves him?

And yet we read, '[God] did not spare his own Son, but gave him up for us all' (v. 32). So along with the pattern of love, we see the paradox of love: it comes at a cost. The love of God for a lost world was at the cost of the sacrifice of his own beloved Son. This should make us stop and reflect: 'As the Father has loved me, so have I loved you.'

In John 15, Jesus continues, 'Now remain in my love. If you keep my commands, you will remain in my love, just as I have kept my Father's commands and remain in his love. I have told you this so that my joy may be in you and that your joy may be complete' (vv. 9–11).

Love brings joy, but love also involves suffering, sacrifice, pain. Love demands obedience. For Jesus, love meant humbling himself, becoming a servant, being obedient, even to death – and that, death on a cross (Philippians 2:5–8). After the resurrection he said, 'As the Father has sent me, I am sending you' (John 20:21).

3 Dimensions of love (1)

Luke 10:25–37

Paul's prayer for the Ephesian church in Ephesians 3:14–21 speaks of being rooted in love, established in love, with power to grasp the dimensions of Christ's love and to know that love. Ultimately, though, its dimensions can never be fully grasped by our finite minds – to know his love in our own experience, and so be filled to the measure of all the fullness of God. This must be our starting point. We begin with God and his amazing love made known to us in Christ.

What about the dimensions of our love? How is God's amazing love to be reciprocated and reflected? When asked by the Pharisees which was the greatest commandment in the law (Matthew 22:34–40), Jesus referred them to Deuteronomy 6:5, linking it with Leviticus 19:18.

Earlier in Luke 10, Jesus linked these two commands in answer to the expert's question. In thinking about the dimensions of love, we begin with the first and greatest command: 'Love the Lord your God.' I don't think we're intended to be overly analytical, attempting to distinguish heart, soul, mind and strength. It's saying: love God with everything you are and with everything you have. Note the repetition of 'all'. Don't hold anything back. In its original Old Testament context, there is a balancing prohibition. Devotion to God calls for the rejection of all false gods.

The second command is also a command to love, a horizontal as well as a vertical dimension: 'Love your neighbour as yourself.' Of course, this prompted the famous question, 'Who is my neighbour?' which Jesus answered by telling a story. When he had finished the story, he also posed a question, a different question, a much more challenging one: 'Which of these three do you think was a neighbour to the man who fell into the hands of robbers?'

Jesus' question is not 'Who is my neighbour?' but 'What kind of neighbour am I?'

A further dimension of the command to love is even more radical: love your enemies (Matthew 5:43–48). Don't hate them; love them, pray for them, treat evil people and good people alike, don't just love those who love you. Characteristically, Jesus puts his challenge in a series of questions climaxing in the searching question, 'What are you doing more than others?'

4 Dimensions of love (2)

John 13:34–35; Ephesians 5:25–33; 1 John 3:16–18

In what sense could Jesus' command to love be a new command? To love God and one's neighbour was not new, but the command given to the twelve represented a new context: 'one another', that is, the fellowship of those who were the followers and friends of Jesus, distinguished from the hostile environment of the world (John 15:18–25; cf. John 17:9). They were a diverse and, one might say, incompatible group, and the evidence in the Gospels of their interactions suggests that this command was not superfluous. A helpful study is the occurrence of 'one another' texts in the epistles. See for example Romans 12:10, 16; 13:8; 14:13; 15:7.

The standard of the love that Jesus commanded was also new: 'as I have loved you'. Jesus not only demanded a life of love from his disciples, he demonstrated it.

In Ephesians 5, Paul identifies a very specific context in which the love command is to be obeyed, when he directs husbands to love their wives. In modern Western culture, we are conditioned to concentrate more on what is meant by wives submitting to their husbands, but it is worth noting that Paul allocated twice as much space to instructing husbands as to wives.

Here's a checklist for husbands based on this passage. What have you given up for your wife? How much do you notice and how appreciative are you? How generous are you towards her? Husbands are to love their wives in the same way as Christ loved the church. A valid translation of verse 27 is 'that he might present the church to himself gorgeous'.

1 John has a lot to say about love, including what not to love (1 John 2:15–17). It is more like a family conference than a letter and it is full of love. The NIV's 'dear children' is more literally 'beloved'. We are used to thinking about love as a feeling, an emotion, but that's not what God means by it. You can love someone without actually liking them. Love is not dependent on whether we 'like' or 'dislike' other people. It has everything to do with how we treat them.

5 Love is the greatest

1 Corinthians 13

This chapter should not be isolated from its context. Paul is teaching about spiritual gifts and in verses 1–3 he reminds us that love is essential. Without love, our gifts are useless. He starts with the exciting, spectacular gift most valued by the Corinthians: speaking in tongues. In verse 2 he moves to the gifts he valued most: prophecy, knowledge and faith. Without love, they are useless. Verse 3 moves to aspects of Christian living which even the world would recognise as valuable, not gifts we receive from God but service we render to God. Without love, even our greatest sacrifice will be fruitless. Without love, I achieve nothing, I am nothing, I gain nothing.

Verses 4–7 explain that love is practical, summed up in 15 characteristics, seven positive and eight negative. The test of our love is the extent to which we can replace 'love/it' with our own names, an exercise to be carried out humbly, honestly and unhurriedly. What makes this standard not just practical but possible is the fact that we can put Christ's name there. Only by abiding in him with his life flowing through us is such fruitfulness possible.

Verses 8–13 reinforce the truth that love is eternal: 'Love never ends' (v. 8, NRSV). Paul uses three analogies to illustrate, first the incomplete and the complete. Some see the 'completeness' of verse 10 as the canon of scripture, but neither Paul nor the Corinthians would have understood it that way. A reference to the future state of the believer in eternity is much more likely. Meanwhile, a spirit of sympathy and humility rather than criticism and pride is in order.

The second analogy (v. 11) is that of the child and the adult. As Christians on earth, we are still children, still growing, learning. We have not yet reached full maturity. Verse 12 contrasts reflection with reality. Mirrors were poor in Paul's day, though Corinth produced some of the best of them. I used to visit a house with an upright piano near the window. The family could tell that someone was at the door from the reflection on the piano, but only when they opened the door could they see exactly who the visitor was.

Faith will become sight; hope will be fulfilled; but love will be for ever.

6 Love's dilemmas and demands

1 Samuel 20:1–17

The story of Jonathan illustrates the dilemmas that love creates. He was a good soldier and a brave one (1 Samuel 14:1–14). At the same time, he had a very loving nature. He loved his father, King Saul, a man with many faults which got worse the older he grew, but Jonathan loved his dad and remained loyal to him to the very end (2 Samuel 1:23). At the same time, Jonathan's loving nature is seen in his love for his friend David and the covenant relationship between them.

So Jonathan is a shining example of love, but here's the problem: Saul hated David. He was jealous of him, afraid of him and, in his worst moments of madness, tried to kill him. Saul tried desperately to get his son to side with him. So Jonathan had to make a decision: whose side was he going to be on? His father's or his friend's?

Saul had no doubt where his loyalty should lie, and so Jonathan was put under enormous pressure to choose. But he couldn't choose and his tender soul was torn apart. Love can tear you apart. God the Father knows what that means: loving his only begotten Son and loving a lost world that rejects his Son. How can we cope when faced with the divided loyalties which other people try to impose upon us?

A New Testament perspective on this dilemma is highlighted in Paul's 'love in action' section in Romans 12:9–21. In verse 18 he writes, 'If it is possible, as far as it depends on you, live at peace with everyone.' There's a command there, but along with the command there are two provisos. Firstly, 'if it is possible'; it may not be. Secondly, 'as far as it depends on you'; it may not ultimately depend on you.

But even if it's not possible and even if it doesn't depend on us, we must keep trying. That was the challenge facing Jonathan, and we may well find ourselves facing the same challenge, particularly in family situations. However difficult, however painful, love demands that we never give up. Love always perseveres. See also Matthew 5:9 and James 3:18.

Guidelines

- Take time to read through 1 John at a single sitting, noting all that is said there about love.
- God is love. We love because he first loved us. It is said that 'hurt people hurt people'. Conversely, loved people love people. The only completely reliable source of unfailing love is God himself. Take time to reflect on how much God loves you and allow it to penetrate your soul.
- What are the practical implications of this fruit of the Spirit in your own life in relation to the past, the present and the future?
- My internet search for 'a prayer for love' brought up mainly prayers relating to romantic love. Write your own prayer to God based on your reflections this week.

20–26 August

1 Joy in Old and New Testaments

Luke 10:13–23

Joy and rejoicing feature throughout the Bible. In the Old Testament, we find joy frequently associated with festive worship, victory in battle and the ingathering of harvest (for example Deuteronomy 16:14–15; Isaiah 9:3).

The theme of joy continues in the New Testament, most prominently in the writings of Luke, John and Paul. Luke's Gospel begins with 'good news that will cause great joy for all the people' (2:10). In chapter 10, when the 72 returned joyfully following their mission, Jesus said, 'Do not rejoice that the spirits submit to you, but rejoice that your names are written in heaven' (10:17, 20). At that time – a time of woe to unrepentant towns – Jesus was nevertheless 'full of joy through the Holy Spirit', praising God his Father (10:13–15, 21). The Gospel climaxes in the return of the disciples to Jerusalem 'with great joy' following Christ's ascension (24:52).

Prominently featured in the book of Acts are the many 'great' things recorded there, among them 'great joy'. There was great joy in a Samaritan city when many experienced deliverance and healing (8:8) and in Pisidian Antioch 'the disciples were filled with joy and with the Holy Spirit' (13:52).

Characteristic of joy in John's Gospel is the idea of fullness or completeness. John the Baptist's joy is likened to that of the bridegroom's friend on hearing the bridegroom's voice (3:29), joy that is 'full' and now 'complete'. In the upper room discourse (13—17), Jesus' intention for the disciples is that his joy may be in them and that their joy may be complete (15:11). In 16:19–24, he contrasts present grief with future joy, likening their experience to that of a woman giving birth, then linking 'complete joy' with answered prayer. This link between joy and prayer is further confirmed in Jesus' prayer to the Father for his disciples: 'I am coming to you now, but I say these things while I am still in the world, so that they may have the full measure of my joy within them' (17:13).

The concepts of 'great' and 'complete' joy reappear in the Johannine letters (1 John 1:4; 2 John 1:4, 12; 3 John 1:3, 4). It was John's aim in writing, joy stimulated by seeing others walking in the truth, and the joy of face to face fellowship. It was characteristically outward, not inward looking.

2 Joy in Philippians

Philippians 4:1–4, 10–20

When Paul wrote to the Philippian Christians, his circumstances were hardly conducive to joy: chained as a Roman prisoner, struggling, not knowing whether life or death awaited him, maligned by rival preachers and heartbroken over many who were living as enemies of the cross of Christ. Yet this letter is suffused with joy. It appears in chapter 1 first: 'I always pray with joy' (1:4–6). This confidence was twofold, based on their partnership in the gospel and the good work God was doing and would continue to do in them (illustrating our part and God's part in his work).

Paul rejoiced in the preaching of the gospel, whether from false motives or true. It was a joy that could see beyond petty jealousies to spiritual realities (1:18–19), fed by a concern for the progress of others more than his own well-being (1:25).

In chapter 2, he encouraged his readers to make his joy complete (2:2), not by providing for his needs (though he was grateful for that; see 4:10–14), but by developing a Christlike mindset, resulting in love, unity and harmony, eradicating selfishness and conceit, encouraging humility and concern for others (2:1–5).

Both Timothy (2:19) and Epaphroditus (2:25–29) could be relied upon to lighten the atmosphere with their joy. Could that be said of us?

Chapter 4 adds further insights. For Paul, the believers are his 'joy and crown' as he urges them to stand firm in the Lord, knowing that they are citizens of heaven (v. 1). Verse 4 throws important light on what Christian joy, the fruit of the Spirit, is all about: like love, it is not merely commended but commanded, and indeed in a repeated command.

We tend to think of joy as a natural expression of emotion, a spontaneous reaction to favourable circumstances. But the command form indicates that it is rather an expression of obedience, a response that we impose on our circumstances, whether good or bad. How can that be possible? The key is the words 'in the Lord' (vv. 1–2, 4, 10). Joy is the fruit of the Spirit, the life of Christ flowing through us when we take authority over our circumstances (note 'always') and are not controlled by them.

3 Peace which only Jesus can give

John 14:1–6, 25–29

In Old Testament contexts, peace can indicate the absence of war (1 Samuel 7:14) but more typically it has the sense of general well-being, the true source of which is the Lord (Numbers 6:24–26) and is closely linked with salvation (Isaiah 52:7). Hebrew idiom uses repetition to express a superlative and Isaiah uses this idiom with reference to the 'perfect peace' of those who truly trust in God (Isaiah 26:3) and who receive his healing (57:19). However, 'there is no peace… for the wicked' (57:21).

In the New Testament, the noun occurs in every book except 1 John. The characteristic greeting at the start of many letters is 'Grace and peace to you from God our Father and the Lord Jesus Christ' (Galatians 1:3), demonstrating both that peace is concomitant with grace and that Jesus, equally with the Father, is its source. The order is significant: first grace and then peace.

Peace is related to joy. It has been said that joy is peace running and peace is joy resting.

The opening words of John 14, 'Do not let your hearts be troubled', are a familiar part of Christian funeral services. In their original context they were spoken only hours before the climax of Passion Week. Jesus spoke of 'my peace… not… as the world gives' and then repeated the command not to be troubled or afraid (v. 27).

What makes this even more poignant is the prayer of Jesus recorded earlier in 12:27–28, where the same language appears: 'Now my soul is troubled, and what shall I say? "Father save me from this hour"? No… Father, glorify your name!' Here we see something of the burden of sin and suffering which Jesus bore on our behalf in order that we might know his peace.

Returning to 14:27, Jesus uses the language of legacy: 'Peace I leave with you.' Following his resurrection, his first words to the disciples were 'Peace be with you!' (John 20:19, 21, 26). Much more than merely a standard greeting, it was the fulfilment of his promise. There have been protracted probate cases where the legacy has been delayed or diminished by the process of law, but this is the only case in history where the person who made the will came back to ensure it was being carried out!

4 Peace which transcends all understanding

Mark 4:35–41; Philippians 4:4–9

Jesus was asleep while a storm threatened to swamp the boat – along with the disciples. He rebuked the wind and waves, then challenged the disciples over their lack of faith. There are two kinds of peace: peace when there is no storm and peace during the storm. The former is easy to understand, a peace that the world can give. Peace while the storm is raging is not; it is 'beyond our utmost understanding' (Philippians 4:4, NEB). This is the peace which Jesus described as 'my peace', which he demonstrated and only he can give.

This quality of peace is described in Philippians 4. Paul was enduring his own stormy circumstances and yet he could experience that supernatural peace which Jesus alone can give. Verses 6–9 outline God's peace formula. It contains both commands and promises. We can only enjoy the promises if we follow the commands, but when we follow the commands the promises are guaranteed.

Verse 6 contains two commands, one negative and the other positive. What should we worry about? Nothing. What should we pray about? Everything. The first command would be ridiculous were it not balanced by the second. Paul describes prayer in four ways, both for emphasis and to express variety in prayer, but always with the gratitude attitude.

Verse 7 contains the first promise, protection from within, like a garrison protecting a town.

Verse 8 contains the third command. The key word is 'think'. Paul presents us with six targets which are not confined to Christian specifics but embrace the 'whatever', followed by two criteria which must control our thinking.

Verse 9 contains the fourth command and the key word is 'do', not this time 'whatever' (although the NIV uses 'whatever' again) but literally 'what'. He is not talking now in general terms but in specifics: education, tradition, instruction and imitation that are specifically Christian. Paul could point to his own example and message (3:17).

The second promise now follows. Note the new element in this promise, not simply the peace of God, as if that were somehow a detachable asset, but the very presence of the God of peace, a peace which can only be experienced as we draw near to God himself and he draws near to us. We know the peace of God by knowing the God of peace and our experience of the God of peace is always 'in Christ Jesus'.

5 Patience

Matthew 18:21–35

The KJV's 'longsuffering' reflects the structure of the noun in the original Greek. The cognate adjective was used in the Greek translation of the Old Testament to represent the characteristic description of Yahweh as 'slow to anger' (e.g. Exodus 34:6). F.F. Bruce coined the term 'long-tempered', as opposed to 'short-tempered', to describe this quality.

This aspect of God's character is picked up in the parable of the unmerciful servant, where the cognate verb is used ('be patient,' vv. 26, 29). God's forbearance is represented in the initial response of the king (v. 27). However, when the servant refused the pleading of his fellow servant, the king's slowness to anger ceased (v. 34). It seems likely from the Old Testament background that dealing with anger is part of this fruit of the Spirit. See also Ephesians 4:26, 31; Colossians 3:8, 13; James 1:19.

Peter reminds us of God's patience in salvation. He is not slow in keeping his promise and does not want any to perish (1 Peter 3:20; 2 Peter 3:9, 15). In Romans, Paul speaks of the riches of God's patience intended to lead to repentance (2:4) and his great patience towards the objects of his wrath (9:22).

Of the 25 occurrences of this word group in the New Testament, about a quarter refer to God's patience. It is clear that when it comes to patience, God is our supreme example but others are cited as examples: Abraham (Hebrews 6:15; cf. 6:12), the prophets (James 5:10), Paul and his co-workers (2 Corinthians 6:4–6; 2 Timothy 3:10). Patience may involve endurance in the face of suffering and is a mark of the true servant of God.

Patience always includes an element of waiting. God waited patiently in the days of Noah. After waiting patiently, Abraham received what was promised. James cites the farmer who waits patiently for the land to yield its valuable crop (5:7). Western culture is conditioned to expect everything instantly, but there is always a time-delay factor involved in patience, for which we need the Holy Spirit's help.

'Clothe yourselves with patience,' Paul writes (Colossians 3:12), indicating that this virtue should be as much a part of us as the clothes we wear. It won't be easy, but in Paul's instruction about dealing with the idle, the disruptive, the disheartened and the weak, his command was 'be patient with everyone' (1 Thessalonians 5:14).

6 Kindness

Genesis 50:15–21

Like patience, kindness is first and foremost a quality displayed by God. The Greek Septuagint translation of Psalm 34:8 is 'Taste and see that the Lord is kind,' quoted by Peter in his first letter (2:3). The adjective *chrēstos*, 'kind', was pronounced similarly to *Christos*, 'Christ', and with this play on words Peter interprets the Old Testament text as an invitation to feed on Christ.

God is 'kind to the ungrateful and wicked' and therefore those who love their enemies, who do good to them, who lend to them without expecting to get anything back, will have a great reward and will be children of the Most High (Luke 6:35).

Kindness and patience are often found together but they are not identical. If patience has mainly to do with an attitude that we develop within ourselves, kindness has everything to do with the actions that we do to and for others. We talk about 'showing' kindness. It can be done secretly, but it will always result in something that is visible, a result that benefits someone other than me.

In Genesis 50, Joseph spoke kindly to his brothers after the death of their father and reassured them. They knew they had treated him badly (compare 37:4). He had tested their loyalty by his apparent mood swings and erratic behaviour on all their famine relief visits and, now that Jacob was dead, it was not unreasonable for them to be afraid. Joseph's depth of feeling is seen in his tears, but his kindness was shown in his words. It is all too possible to be doing acts of apparent kindness but with a bitter spirit and with words that are far from kind. Kindness in action unaccompanied by kind words is no kindness at all. A kind word relieves anxiety, according to Proverbs 12:25, and unless word and action are in agreement, anxiety is likely to remain.

It was a refusal to embrace kindness that led to the disastrous split in the kingdom when King Rehoboam spurned the advice of his older counsellors and opted instead for an increase in cruelty (2 Chronicles 10:7, 13–14.).

Kindness to the poor and needy is particularly emphasised in Proverbs (14:21, 31; 19:17; 28:8). In an unusual proverb, God indicates that right behaviour embraces animals as well as humans: 'The righteous care for the needs of their animals, but the kindest acts of the wicked are cruel' (12:10).

Guidelines

- How would you define happiness? Does it differ from the spiritual fruit of joy and if so how do they differ?
- What things in your life are stressful or painful? How can you apply the command to 'rejoice in the Lord' in these circumstances?
- In John 14, Jesus offered the disciples 'my peace' and commanded, 'Do not let your hearts be troubled.' Yet earlier he had said, 'Now my soul is troubled' (12:27). Paul counselled the Philippians, 'Do not be anxious about anything' (4:6) and yet earlier he had said he wanted to send Epaphroditus back to them 'so that… I may have less anxiety' (2:28). What do these apparent anomalies teach us?
- We may need patience with people, with circumstances, with plans and even with ourselves. Patience is not so much about waiting as how we wait. What distinguishes this fruit of the Spirit from impatience?
- 'Sometimes you have to be cruel to be kind.' What do people mean by that and can it ever be a valid interpretation of biblical kindness?

1 Goodness

Matthew 19:16–26

Although the noun Paul uses in Galatians 5:22 occurs only four times in the New Testament, the concept of goodness permeates the Bible, particularly through the adjective 'good', which occurs over 600 times. While philosophers may debate the precise nature of goodness, scripture affirms that God is good (Psalm 106:1) and is the source of all that is genuinely good. In the creation account, God saw all that he had made and it was very good (Genesis 1:31; cf. 1 Timothy 4:4).

Jesus affirmed the unique goodness of God in his reply to the question about eternal life. The parallels in Mark 10 and Luke 18 show Jesus questioning the enquirer's address ('good teacher') and forcing him to think not only about the nature of goodness but the identity of Jesus himself.

It is important to take note of Isaiah 5:20: 'Woe to those who call evil good and good evil.' Even bad people can be capable of good things. But for sinners who are estranged from God, absolute goodness is impossible, hence Paul, quoting Psalm 14:1–3, writes, 'There is no one who does good, not even one' (Romans 3:12). All are in need of God's saving grace that comes by faith in Christ and the power of his indwelling Spirit.

Believers are God's handiwork, created in Christ Jesus to do good works (Ephesians 2:10). The fruit of the Spirit dominates Paul's prayer for the Colossians. Through a knowledge of God's will, through all the wisdom and understanding that the Spirit gives, we may live a life worthy of the Lord and please him in every way: bearing fruit in every good work, growing in the knowledge of God (Colossians 1:9–12).

This practical emphasis on *doing* good is reinforced in 1 Thessalonians 5:15; 2 Thessalonians 3:13; 1 Timothy 6:18; 1 Peter 2:15, 20; 3:16–17. One of the criteria for elders/overseers in Titus 1:8 goes a step further and includes *loving* what is good. It is possible to do what is good, but grudgingly and reluctantly; that is not God's way. Financial giving should be a result of careful preparation and a generous spirit, not something 'grudgingly given' (2 Corinthians 9:5, 8). Exercising pastoral leadership in the church involves genuine caring, 'not because you must, but because you are willing, as God wants you to be… eager to serve' (1 Peter 5:2).

2 Faithfulness

Matthew 25:14–30

In contrast to 'goodness', this noun occurs over 240 times in the New Testament, especially frequent in the writings of Paul. Depending on the context, it can indicate 'faith' in the sense of trust expressed in commitment (Ephesians 2:8), or 'faithfulness' in the sense of reliability and loyalty (Revelation 13:10), or occasionally 'the faith', that is, the body of Christian teaching (1 Timothy 4:6) or the Christian life itself (1 Timothy 6:10). So which is it here?

Faith is a key concept in Galatians. Justification is by faith in Christ Jesus and not by works of the law. It is this sense that dominates the letter. However, almost without exception, modern English translations opt for 'faithfulness' in Galatians 5:22, which fits the immediate context much better.

This quality is yet again a characteristic of God. 'Great is your faithfulness' (Lamentations 3:23) is one of the strongest affirmations of God's faithfulness in the Old Testament. It is remarkable that it should be made at arguably the lowest point in Israel's history, when kingdom, capital and temple had been destroyed and the people who had been so miraculously delivered from slavery in Egypt had now been so mercilessly driven into exile in Babylon. Yet this truth shines like a beacon in the darkest hour.

In 1 Corinthians, Paul reminds us that the God who called us into fellowship with his Son is faithful. He will keep us firm to the end, so that we will be blameless on the day of our Lord Jesus Christ (1:7–9; cf. 1 Thessalonians 5:23–24). He is faithful in helping us when we are tempted (10:13; cf. 2 Thessalonians 3:1–3).

Jesus pronounced a woe on the teachers of the law and Pharisees for meticulously tithing ridiculously small amounts but neglecting the more important matters of the law, 'justice, mercy and faithfulness' (Matthew 23:23).

In the parable of the bags of gold, it was the 'good and faithful' servants who were commended and invited to share their master's happiness. Our gifts and opportunities will differ but we will be judged by faithfulness in using what we have, not what we don't have.

Another area where we are called to be faithful is prayer (Romans 12:12). In this, Paul is a great example. He could write to the Colossians, 'We have not stopped praying for you' (1:9).

3 Gentleness: meek but not weak

Matthew 21:1–5, 12–17

'The fruit of the Spirit is... gentleness.' The older translation of this word is 'meekness'. Though it sounds like weakness, it means the opposite: strength, but strength under control, controlled by God's Spirit. A police horse in the middle of a riot is not weak. With one strike of its powerful hoof, it could maim or kill, but it doesn't because its strength is under the control of its handler.

This word has a threefold aspect with different nuances depending on the context: 'submissive' referring to our relationship with God; 'gentle' referring to our relationship with other people; and 'humble' referring to the way we think about ourselves.

'The man Moses was very meek' (Numbers 12:3, ESV). He was facing opposition and criticism, even from his own family, but he didn't react unwisely. He was submissive, gentle and humble. His strength was under control. What a contrast to his earlier behaviour in Egypt (Exodus 2:11–12), when he killed an Egyptian and his strength was out of control.

This quality of gentleness characterises God himself. In 1 Kings 19, when Elijah was having a nervous breakdown, God's prescription was a proper meal and a good rest (vv. 5–7). Finally God's presence was revealed, not in the violence of wind, earthquake and fire, but in 'a gentle whisper' (vv. 11–12). He is the God who answers by fire but he is also the God of the gentle whisper.

As always, Jesus reveals the true nature of God. In Matthew 11:29 he says, 'Learn from me, for I am gentle and humble in heart.' When we do, we discover both a rest for our souls and a 'yoke' for our backs, but a yoke that fits easily and a burden that is light.

Towards the end of the period of Old Testament revelation the prophet Zechariah announced the coming of Zion's king: 'See, your king comes to you, righteous and victorious, lowly [gentle] and riding on a donkey, on a colt, the foal of a donkey' (9:9).

Following Christ's triumphal entry to Jerusalem, he overturned the tables of the money changers and the benches of those selling doves. That was not weakness, nor was it violence, but strength – strength under control, submission to God and his will. Yet with that same quality, he brought healing to the blind and the lame and encouragement to the boisterous children.

4 Gentleness 'hot spots'

1 Peter 3:1–16

Paul had much to say about gentleness. He wrote to the Philippians, 'Let your gentleness be evident to all' (4:5). To the Ephesians he wrote, 'Be completely humble and gentle' (4:2). To the Colossians he wrote, 'Clothe yourselves with… gentleness' (3:12). In his first letter to Timothy, he instructed him to 'pursue … gentleness' (6:11) and reminded him that a Christian leader should be 'not violent but gentle' (3:3).

Gentleness should be unmissable, consistent, as obvious as the clothes we are wearing and right up there as one of our biggest ambitions.

There are certain areas where this quality is particularly important. The first is in the words we say and how we say them. 'A gentle answer turns away wrath, but a harsh word stirs up anger' (Proverbs 15:1). Words can wound as well as heal.

A subset of that is the way we speak to people who do not share our faith, even people antagonistic to our faith. We are to be prepared to give an answer 'always' and 'to everyone' but to do this 'with gentleness and respect' (1 Peter 3:15). Opponents must be 'gently instructed' (2 Timothy 2:25).

Another gentleness 'hot spot' is dealing with children. Nowhere is this more evident than in the way Jesus welcomed children and communicated with them. Children can be frustrating and exasperating, but harshness is never the answer. A subset of this is the way we deal with those who are young in the faith. Paul wrote, 'We were like young children [*or* gentle] among you. Just as a nursing mother cares for her children, so we cared for you' (1 Thessalonians 2:7–8).

Another particular area is restoring a Christian who has fallen into sin. Writing to the Galatians, Paul went on to say, 'Brothers and sisters, if someone is caught in a sin, you who live by the Spirit should restore that person gently' (6:1). The word 'restore' is used of the disciples 'mending' their nets. It was also the word used for setting a broken bone. Lives broken by sin need to be put together again. The problem has to be dealt with thoroughly, but the person has to be treated gently.

Unusually, gentleness is also presented as a beauty treatment. In 1 Peter, instruction is given to wives specifically: 'Your beauty… should be that of your inner self, the unfading beauty of a gentle and quiet spirit, which is of great worth in God's sight' (1 Peter 3:3–4).

5 Self-control and temperance

Genesis 9:20–25; 19:30–36

'Self-control' is used to translate a range of words in the original text of the New Testament. The word Paul uses in Galatians 5:23 is derived from a word meaning power. We tend to think of power as something which is exercised over other people, but in this context it means power over ourselves.

Self-control was an ideal in Greek and Roman culture. Athletes trained and disciplined themselves, avoiding everything that might compromise their fitness. These were the popular heroes, just as they are for many today.

This particular word occurs just four times in the New Testament. If we add to the noun the associated adjective and verb, the tally rises to seven. Other words are translated 'self-control' but even with these the maximum is 32. Compare that to the main word for love. With the associated adjective and verb, its tally comes to 320. There are few references, relatively speaking, to self-control.

The reason may be the way it was understood in contemporary culture, where it carried the idea of self-sufficiency, that nothing was impossible to the human spirit if you just took yourself in hand. It was basically a humanistic ideal.

In contrast, the whole message of God's word is that this is exactly what we are not capable of doing. Paul summed it up in Romans 7:18: 'I have the desire to do what is good, but I cannot carry it out.' That's our dilemma, and why we can only experience this kind of self-control with God's help and in God's way. The power we need is God's power, the fruit of the Spirit.

The older translation 'temperance' suggests self-control in the area of strong drink. While drinking alcohol is not forbidden in the Bible, the dangers of drunkenness are made clear. Noah and Lot, both described as 'righteous' men, illustrate the sordid and shameful results when drink robbed them of self-control.

Paul wrote, 'Do not get drunk on wine, which leads to debauchery. Instead, be filled with the Spirit' (Ephesians 5:18); 'Let us be awake and sober' (1 Thessalonians 5:6); and he listed 'drunkenness, orgies and the like' among the acts of the flesh which contrast so strongly with the fruit of the Spirit (Galatians 5:21).

Alcoholism is an addiction, but it is not the only one. Anything becomes an addiction when you no longer control it, but it controls you.

6 Self-control and sexual attraction

2 Samuel 11:1–17

This passage illustrates two aspects of self-control in relation to sexuality. We have David, the God-appointed king, who failed miserably. Then we have Uriah the Hittite – the foreigner, the non-Israelite – whose integrity was unblemished. One lacked self-control. The other displayed remarkable self-control. How did David, of all people, get it so wrong?

It began when he was alone. Being alone can make you vulnerable to temptation. It began when he was idle: 'One evening David got up from his bed' (v. 2).

It began with a neglect of clear duty. It was the time when kings go off to war. David was a king and it was a time of war. It was his clear duty to be with his men, but he sent Joab with the king's men and the army. Every man who had a duty was doing his duty, every man except David.

It began in the evening. There are times and places when we are more susceptible to temptation. A look turned into lust. David took steps to find out more about this woman. The information he was given should have stopped him there and then. She was married. But David had given in so many times by now, he couldn't stop himself. He sent for her and slept with her. Soon news came that he didn't want to hear: she was pregnant.

David debased and disgraced himself still further, embarking on a plan of deceit, sending for Bathsheba's husband so that he would think the baby was his. But Uriah was a noble man, dedicated to his duty, a man with a conscience and a commitment to what was right and proper. Although David did everything he could to encourage Uriah to spend the night with his wife, he refused.

It was not enough that David should do the wrong thing himself. He was determined to get himself off the hook by forcing someone else to do the wrong thing, and so the temptation that led to lust, to deceit, and to enticement finally led to murder.

We live in an age of explicit images in films and adverts, explicit storylines in books and magazines. Fashions are provocative and revealing. Contraception is readily available. The pressure to commit sin in this area is very great and we need the power of God's Holy Spirit to overcome temptation. For a New Testament persective, see 1 Thessalonians 4:3–8.

Guidelines

Theologians distinguish between the communicable and incommunicable attributes of God. There is a tendency to focus on the latter: omnipotence, omniscience, omnipresence, and so on. This can result in a rather cold and impersonal view of God. The fruit of the Spirit encourages us to think of God in 'warmer', more personal terms and reminds us that God is not only able to communicate his nature to us but wants to do so (see 2 Peter 1:3–4).

Review the nine aspects of the fruit of the Spirit, giving thanks for the development of these in your life and seeking God's help honestly and prayerfully where these are lacking.

FURTHER READING

Selwyn Hughes, *Fruit of the Spirit: Growing more like Jesus* (CWR, 2005).

Hazel Offner, *Lifebuilder: Fruit of the Spirit* (Scripture Union, 1999).

Derek Prime, *Living for God's Pleasure: The fruit of the Spirit* (Evangelical Press, 2004).

Christopher J.H. Wright, *Cultivating the Fruit of the Spirit: Growing in Christlikeness* (IVP, 2017).

Overleaf... Guidelines forthcoming issue | Author profile |
Recommended reading | Order and subscription forms

Guidelines forthcoming issue

DAVID SPRIGGS

I hope that you are looking forward to the next issue of *Guidelines* for September–December 2018: I certainly am.

We have a number of new writers, and I am especially pleased that we have two new female ones. These are Miriam Hinksman and Fiona Gregson.

Originally from New Zealand, Miriam came to the UK in 2012 to join the faculty as lecturer in Old Testament at London School of Theology, where she is now a visiting lecturer and associate research fellow. Miriam is married to James and they live in Canterbury with their small daughter.

Her PhD dissertation was on Lamentations. She has also jointly edited a collection of essays reflecting on the role and practice of lament in the church, which became a particularly poignant project in the wake of the Christchurch earthquakes. She is especially interested in how the biblical text can give voice and hope to people of faith today, and takes an active role in teaching and preaching at her local church. For us, she is turning her attention to Obadiah and Nahum.

Fiona Gregson is an ordained Anglican whose UK ministry has been mainly in inner-city multicultural parishes. Fiona is based in the Diocese of Birmingham and splits her time between the church, teaching, writing and caring for her young daughter. She has also lived and worked in several African countries. These experiences motivate her concern for Christian engagement with poverty and possessions.

Her research is mainly in the area of sharing and possessions in the New Testament. In her PhD, she examined six diverse New Testament examples of sharing in their historical and cultural contexts. She then compared them to non-Christian examples to identify similarities and differences. She identified common characteristics across the New Testament examples and consistent distinctives in how the early church shared possessions compared to the surrounding cultures.

We can therefore expect to be given insight and challenge as she takes us to some important New Testament texts that deal with this topic. There

will be added significance for us as we approach the Christmas season, with its emphasis on giving and receiving.

We are also privileged to have two male writers who are new to *Guidelines*. Paul Bradbury has written a book on vocation for BRF and he will be sharing his understanding with us. This is a vital part of our discipleship, spirituality and mission, and also frequently our role as leaders. We will have much to gain from his insights. Paul Jones has researched the spirituality of the prophets and will engage with six prophets to stimulate our own relationship with God.

Jeremy Duff will share with us his understanding of gender issues within the Bible – aspects of which can challenge and distress people in our churches. Andrew Lincoln encourages us by looking at 'human flourishing' in John's Gospel, while Kate Bruce challenges us with the issues within the book of Lamentations.

As Steve Motyer brings his fascinating exposition on Mark 1—8 to an end, Steve Walton is preparing next year to unpack the next lectionary Gospel – Luke. In this issue he will prepare us for this as he looks at the early part of Luke's Gospel with Advent in mind. I will also offer an Advent contribution by exploring different 'special births' throughout the Bible which will amplify the significance of the birth of Jesus.

This looks to be the kind of issue which will bring splashes of God-light into all our lives.

Author profile: Graham Dow

Daily Bible reading began for me on the day of my conversion, aged twelve. The counsellor at the Billy Graham rally in 1955 gave me a packet of Bible verses. Some are among my favourites: 'How can a young man cleanse his way? By taking heed according to your word... Your word I have hidden in my heart, that I might not sin against you' (Psalm 119:9, 11, NKJV).

My teenage nurture in the faith came through a Crusader Bible class. Questions were encouraged and the Bible turned to. A fifties Crusader motto is another of my favourites, 'Trust in the Lord with all your heart, and lean not on your own understanding (Proverbs 3:5, NIV).

To take the whole Bible as the word of God was not a difficult decision. Alternatives were far worse. We can only know God through his revelation of himself. A selective approach to scripture will be affected by what the culture at the time finds thinkable. Very unsatisfactory. It is better to say I don't fully understand a passage than to reject its authority. I studied biblical theology at degree level and loved it. I don't meet any attacks on the Bible's authority that I haven't thought about, and I don't expect the ancient scriptures to match 21st-century patterns of acceptable behaviour.

The history of the people of God is a history of promises. Scripture promises have long been central to my faith. From student days I have thrown my weight on John 15:16, saying that Jesus has chosen me to bear lasting fruit. I was assured of the life of the Holy Spirit in me by taking Luke 11:13 as a promise, not just an optimistic hope. I believe God's 'precious and very great promises' give me a share in his divine life (2 Peter 1:4, ESV).

Romans has taught me to live by grace, not by striving. Revelation has taught me how evil works in society. Ephesians 4 shows me the fivefold ministry necessary for a growing church. I find in the Psalms almost every mood I experience.

In my early nurture, I was taught that we were to follow the teaching of Jesus given to the first disciples. But I never thought to ask, 'Why, then, are we not doing healing ministry?' Subsequently, it has become very important to me to show the kingdom of God in practice as well as in words.

So I commend the continuing, thoughtful engagement with scripture that *Guidelines* encourages.

An extract from *A Guide to Mission Accompaniment*

Accompaniment. It is friendship, but it's more than that. It is mentoring, with a crucial aim.

In this unique book on the subject, Kerry Thorpe argues that Christian accompaniment is a continuing relationship that helps those involved to function better in the things they do. He encourages church leaders and others engaged in mission to develop relationships that inspire, motivate and focus on the church's task of mission. Here is a book that will transform the life of the church. The following extract is taken from the first chapter.

I had no idea what to do. It felt overwhelming. I don't think I had any illusions about full-time ministry being a bed of roses, but this was way beyond anything that I had anticipated. Like so many of my colleagues before and since, I found myself asking if I had in any way been adequately prepared for what I now faced. Life, never mind ministry, makes demands. It is an inescapable component of the human condition to find ourselves confronted by challenges that look to be hopelessly beyond our capabilities. This, for me, was where the story of relational accompaniment starts.

I had spent four years in theological college. Previously riding racehorses for a living and later qualifying as an embalmer in the funeral trade had taught me much about life (and its opposite). Now I had a degree in theology to add to the resources. This was my first curacy, and a role as a junior member of a large staff team in as busy a parish church as could be found in the late 1970s. One thousand people per week came through the doors to multiple services, community events and children's work that spanned all ages. My specific responsibility was for the teenagers. There was already a flourishing group, between 20 and 50 strong, that well predated my arrival.

Now the vicar had taken ill. Roy Barker, the much-loved man in charge, was no longer on the scene. After 18 years of transforming mission, the team leader and driving force was suddenly absent. This was the unantici-

pated crisis in what already looked like a massive challenge. It was clearly going to be all hands on deck. The remaining four full-time staff would have to share out responsibilities. The neat division of labour so far envisaged would be shot to pieces. Much more would be needed of us. (No one knew how long this was going to last. In the event, the vicar was ill for about a year. Then he announced a move and the parish was in interregnum. Finally, a new appointment was made, and quite naturally the new man needed adequate time to discern his own priorities. All in all, the situation continued for about three years.) This was going to be not so much a crisis, more a way of life.

So, how could we continue to see growth? How would we conserve the gains already made? Or, more realistically, how might we even survive?

For me, the great insight that would urge me on through the next 40 years of ministry was born not out of a deeply spiritual season of prayer and discernment, nor out of a highly structured management planning session, but out of crisis, out of sheer desperation.

The only sustainable way forward that I could envisage would need other people, many other people. If they had already known what to do, then presumably they would have been doing it by now. This was going to require some fresh thinking. It would mean breaking new ground and many of us doing what we had not previously imagined. More people involved, more gifts harnessed, new skills developed and old reluctance and barriers overcome.

From where would this amazing army of volunteers emerge? How could we recruit, train, develop and support a brand-new tranche of effective leaders? The answer was quite simply that we couldn't. That would be a dream too far. We would have to work with what we had already got. And that was it. That was the breakthrough.

My main responsibility was for that blossoming group of teenagers. They were of course as remarkable, capable, trying, disruptive and annoying as any bunch of kids that you might wish to meet. Within the pack were some natural leaders. There were others who might be encouraged to develop those gifts. There were kids with bright ideas and some who could just as easily be trouble. They were capable of great disruption, or perhaps they were young adults just waiting to blossom. Either way, they were potential on legs.

Sheer survival determined that there would be little time to run anything like a selection process for what lay ahead. My wife and I, with two

other couples from the congregation to help, sat down with our list of teenage participants. We prayed, of course we prayed. Then we simply divided up the list into groups, using our scant knowledge of personalities and proclivities. Within each group we identified a potential peer-group leader. For each leader we nominated an associate from within that same group. To each group we allocated one of the adult couples as support. And so, for us, the concept of relational mission accompaniment was born. In effect, the teens themselves would do the ministry. They would run the small group meetings. They would keep in touch with each other between times. We would provide the support. We could never have given adequate personal attention to a group of 50 or so youngsters, but we could, between us, help to develop significantly five or ten individuals. That is exactly what we did.

Lesson learned

This short, headline-grabbing story shows that three years later, those three groups of ten or twelve had grown to ten such units. The 30 to 50 had become somewhere around 100 plus. There were large-scale Sunday evening gatherings for the whole crowd, but life, support, mission and growth happened in those smaller, peer-led, relational groupings. The adults focused almost entirely on supporting the young emerging leaders.

It must be stressed that this was not initially a strategy for growth. It was a bunch of fallible human beings adopting a high-risk approach in a bid for sheer survival. It laid the foundation for what I later discovered alluded to by William James, the founder of modern sociology and chronicler of spiritual experience:

I am done with great things and big plans, great institutions and big success. I am for those tiny, invisible loving human forces that work from individual to individual, creeping through the crannies of the world like so many rootlets, or like the capillary oozing of water, which, if given time, will rend the hardest monuments of pride.

William James, *The Letters of William James*, ed. Henry James (1926), vol. 2, p. 90

There is, quite naturally, a mass of detail, trial and error, failure as well as success behind the headline story of our Merseyside youth work. But the principle holds absolutely firm. What could *not* have been achieved by a single individual became flourishing, sustainable mission and

growth when more and more individuals were developed, supported and accompanied through their own burgeoning ministry. At the heart of it, the one individual whose story I am most qualified to tell escaped burnout, survived inordinate pressure and flourished. Giving ministry away, releasing the gifts and callings of other people and, above all, concentrating on a relational mission accompaniment was going to shape my approach to the multiplicity of missional challenges that the next 40 years would bring.

To order a copy of this book, please turn to the order form on page 149.

Recommended reading

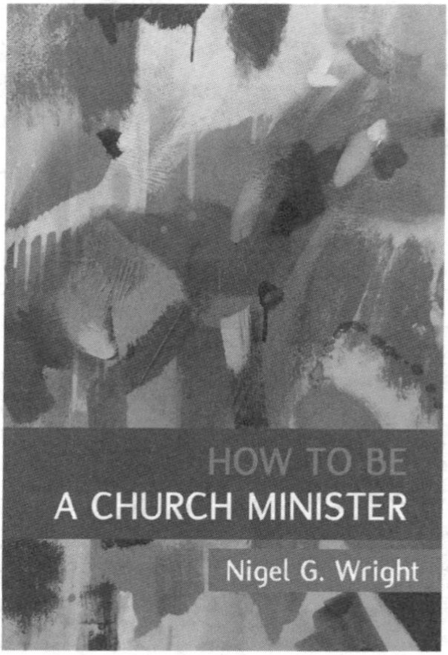

This timely book sets out what is involved in being a Christian minister – its joys and challenges, its responsibilities and privileges. It discusses the call to and the work of ministry. It will enable you to understand your calling more fully and inform your practice. It will stimulate careful and biblical reflection. *How to Be a Church Minister* is set to be a seminal volume on the subject.

How to Be a Church Minister
Nigel G. Wright
978 0 85746 689 1 £12.99
brfonline.org.uk

A Franciscan Way of Life
Brother Ramon's quest for holiness
ARTHUR HOWELLS
Foreword by David Winter

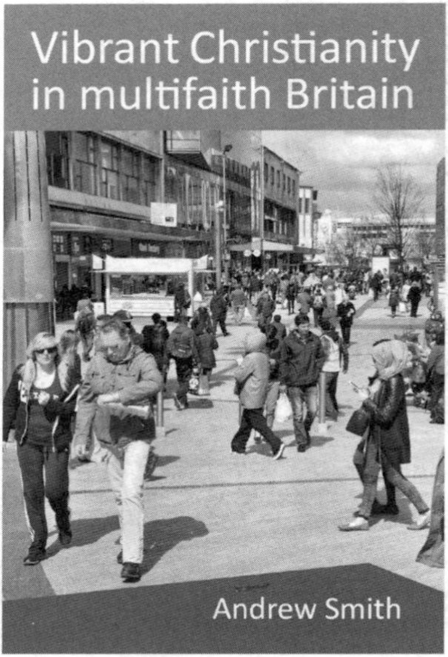

Equipping the church for a faithful engagement with people of different faiths, *Vibrant Christianity in Multifaith Britain* is an accessible and thought-provoking approach that encourages readers to think seriously about how we live out our faith in an increasingly multifaith society. Whether we meet people of different faiths or just hear about them in the media, this book will give Christians confidence to express our faith in a religiously diverse world.

Vibrant Christianity in Multifaith Britain
Andrew Smith
978 0 85746 571 9 £7.99
brfonline.org.uk

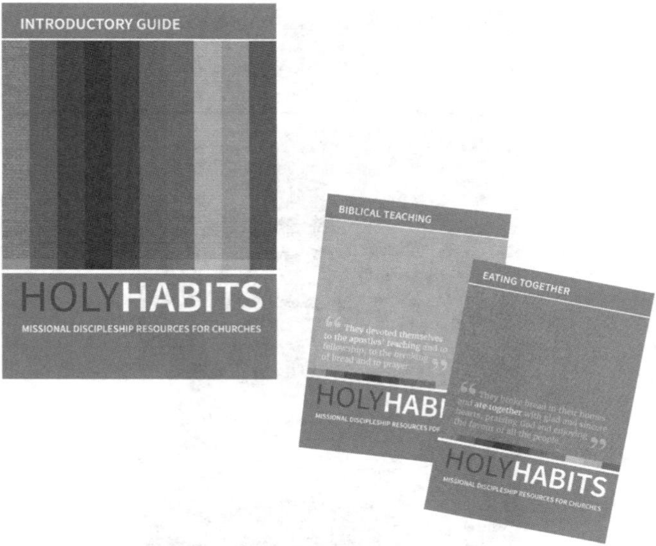

Holy Habits is an initiative to nurture Christian discipleship. It explores Luke's model of church found in Acts 2:42–47, identifies ten habits and encourages the development of a way of life formed by them. These full-colour resources have been developed to help churches explore the habits in worship and other group activities and live out the habits in whole-life, missional discipleship.

Holy Habits

Missional discipleship resources for churches

978 0 85746 677 8 £4.99 (Introductory Guide)

brfonline.org.uk

TITLES IN THE **HOLY HABITS** SERIES:

Biblical Teaching
978 0 85746 678 5 £4.99

Fellowship
978 0 85746 679 5 £4.99

Breaking Bread
978 0 85746 680 8 £4.99

Prayer
978 0 85746 681 5 £4.99

Sharing Resources
978 0 85746 682 2 £4.99

Serving
978 0 85746 683 9 £4.99

Eating Together
978 0 85746 684 6 £4.99

Gladness and Generosity
978 0 85746 685 3 £4.99

Worship
978 0 85746 686 0 £4.99

Making More Disciples
978 0 85746 687 7 £4.99

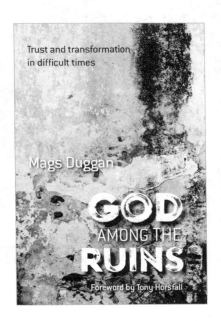

To order

Online: **brfonline.org.uk**
Telephone: +44 (0)1865 319700
Mon–Fri 9.15–17.30

Delivery times within the UK are normally 15 working days. Prices are correct at the time of going to press but may change without prior notice.

BRF

Please return this form to:
BRF
15 The Chambers
Vineyard, Abingdon OX14 3FE
enquiries@brf.org.uk

POSTAGE & PACKING CHARGES	
Order value	**UK**
Under £7.00	£2.00
£7.00–£29.99	£3.00
£30.00 and over	FREE
Order value	**Europe**
Under £7.00	£5.00
£7.00–£29.99	£9.00
£30.00 and over	£9.00 + 15% of order value
Order value	**Rest of world**
Under £7.00	£7.00
£7.00–£29.99	£15.00
£30.00 and over	£15.00 + 20% of order value

Title	Price	Qty	Total
A Guide to Mission Accompaniment	£7.99		
How to Be a Church Minister	£12.99		
A Franciscan Way of Life	£8.99		
Vibrant Christianity in Multifaith Britain	£7.99		
Holy Habits: Introductory Guide	£4.99		
Holy Habits: Biblical Teaching	£4.99		
Holy Habits: Fellowship	£4.99		
Holy Habits: Breaking Bread	£4.99		
Holy Habits: Prayer	£4.99		
Holy Habits: Sharing Resources	£4.99		
Holy Habits: Serving	£4.99		
Holy Habits: Eating Together	£4.99		
Holy Habits: Gladness and Generosity	£4.99		
Holy Habits: Worship	£4.99		
Holy Habits: Making More Disciples	£4.99		
God Among the Ruins	£7.99		

Total value of books	
Postage & packing	
Total for this order	

To read our terms and find out about cancelling your order, please visit brfonline.org.uk/terms.

Please complete in BLOCK CAPITALS

Title .... First name/initials .... Surname ....

Address ....

.... Postcode ....

Acc. No. .... Telephone ....

Email ....

❑ Please keep me informed by email about BRF's books and resources
❑ Please keep me informed by email about the wider work of BRF

Method of payment

❑ Cheque (made payable to BRF) ❑ MasterCard / Visa

Card no. ☐☐☐☐ ☐☐☐☐ ☐☐☐☐ ☐☐☐☐

Valid from M M Y Y Expires M M Y Y Security code* ☐☐☐
Last 3 digits on the reverse of the card

Signature* .... Date .... /........ /........

*ESSENTIAL IN ORDER TO PROCESS YOUR ORDER

The Bible Reading Fellowship (BRF) is a Registered Charity (233280)

GL0218

How to encourage Bible reading in your church

BRF has been helping individuals connect with the Bible for over 90 years. We want to support churches as they seek to encourage church members into regular Bible reading.

Order a Bible reading resources pack

This pack is designed to give your church the tools to publicise our Bible reading notes. It includes:

- Sample Bible reading notes for your congregation to try.
- Publicity resources, including a poster.
- A church magazine feature about Bible reading notes.

The pack is free, but we welcome a £5 donation to cover the cost of postage. If you require a pack to be sent outside the UK or require a specific number of sample Bible reading notes, please contact us for postage costs. More information about what the current pack contains is available on our website.

How to order and find out more

- Visit **biblereadingnotes.org.uk/for-churches**
- Telephone BRF on +44 (0)1865 319700 Mon–Fri 9.15–17.30
- Write to us at BRF, 15 The Chambers, Vineyard, Abingdon OX14 3FE

Keep informed about our latest initiatives

We are continuing to develop resources to help churches encourage people into regular Bible reading, wherever they are on their journey. Join our email list at **biblereadingnotes.org.uk/helpingchurches** to stay informed about the latest initiatives that your church could benefit from.

Introduce a friend to our notes

We can send information about our notes and current prices for you to pass on. Please contact us.

BRF Transforming lives and communities

BRF is a charity that is passionate about making a difference through the Christian faith. We want to see lives and communities transformed through our creative programmes and resources for individuals, churches and schools. We are doing this by resourcing:

- **Christian growth and understanding of the Bible.** Through our Bible reading notes, books, digital resources, Quiet Days and other events, we're resourcing individuals, groups and leaders in churches for their own spiritual journey and for their ministry.
- **Church outreach in the local community.** BRF is the home of three programmes that churches are embracing to great effect as they seek to engage with their local communities: Messy Church, Who Let The Dads Out? and The Gift of Years.
- **Teaching Christianity in primary schools.** Our Barnabas in Schools team is working with primary-aged children and their teachers, enabling them to explore Christianity creatively and confidently within the school curriculum.
- **Children's and family ministry.** Through our Parenting for Faith programme, websites and published resources, we're working with churches and families, enabling children and adults alike to explore Christianity creatively and bring the Bible alive.

Do you share our vision?

Sales of our books and Bible reading notes cover the cost of producing them. However, our other programmes are funded primarily by donations, grants and legacies. If you share our vision, would you help us to transform even more lives and communities? Your prayers and financial support are vital for the work that we do.

- You could support BRF's ministry with a one-off gift or regular donation (using the response form on page 153).
- You could consider making a bequest to BRF in your will (page 152).
- You could encourage your church to support BRF as part of your church's giving to home mission – perhaps focusing on a specific area of our ministry, or a particular member of our Barnabas in Schools team.
- Most important of all, you could support BRF with your prayers.

Make a lasting difference through a gift in your will

The humble match is a wonder of modern invention. Since the dawn of time, humanity had tried to create and harness fire, but nobody came close to finding a reliable self-igniting source until 1805, when the first match was struck. Now just a quick flick along a rough surface is enough to create a spark. Under the right conditions, it grows into a powerful fire.

BRF's story began in a similar way in 1922, with a spark of an idea and the vision of just one man. Revd Leslie Mannering wanted to help his congregation 'get a move on spiritually'. His idea spread like wildfire and soon BRF was born, a charity committed to transforming lives and communities through the Christian faith.

With God's help, we've fanned the flames for over 90 years and have seen our impact grow. Today we are home to four programmes that churches worldwide are embracing as they seek to engage with local communities and transform lives: Messy Church, The Gift of Years, Who Let The Dads Out? and Parenting for Faith. Messy Church in particular is an outstanding success story. Our network of nearly 4,000 Messy Churches reaches an estimated 500,000 people each month with the good news of Jesus Christ.

If you share our passion for making a difference through the Christian faith, would you consider leaving a gift to BRF in your will? Gifts in wills are an important source of income for us and they don't need to be huge to make a real difference. For every £1 we receive, we invest 95p back into charitable activities. Just imagine what we could do over the next century with your help.

For further information about making a gift to BRF in your will, please visit **brf.org.uk/lastingdifference**, contact Sophie Aldred on **+44 (0)1865 319700** or email **giving@brf.org.uk**.

Whatever you can do or give, we thank you for your support.

SHARING OUR VISION – MAKING A GIFT

I would like to make a gift to support BRF. Please use my gift for:

☐ where it is needed most ☐ Barnabas in Schools ☐ Parenting for Faith

☐ Messy Church ☐ Who Let The Dads Out? ☐ The Gift of Years

Title	First name/initials	Surname
Address		
		Postcode
Email		
Telephone		
Signature		Date

giftaid it You can add an extra 25p to every £1 you give.

Please treat as Gift Aid donations all qualifying gifts of money made

☐ today, ☐ in the past four years, ☐ and in the future.

I am a UK taxpayer and understand that if I pay less Income Tax and/or Capital Gains Tax in the current tax year than the amount of Gift Aid claimed on all my donations, it is my responsibility to pay any difference.

☐ My donation does not qualify for Gift Aid.

Please notify BRF if you want to cancel this Gift Aid declaration, change your name or home address, or no longer pay sufficient tax on your income and/or capital gains.

Please complete other side of form ➔

Please return this form to:

BRF, 15 The Chambers, Vineyard, Abingdon OX14 3FE

BRF

The Bible Reading Fellowship is a Registered Charity (233280)

SHARING OUR VISION – MAKING A GIFT

Regular giving

By Direct Debit:

☐ I would like to make a regular gift of £ ______ per month/quarter/year.
Please also complete the Direct Debit instruction on page 159.

By Standing Order:

Please contact Priscilla Kew +44 (0)1235 462305 | giving@brf.org.uk

One-off donation

Please accept my gift of:

☐ £10 ☐ £50 ☐ £100 Other £ ______

by (delete as appropriate):

☐ Cheque/Charity Voucher payable to 'BRF'

☐ MasterCard/Visa/Debit card/Charity card

Name on card

Card no. ☐☐☐☐ ☐☐☐☐ ☐☐☐☐ ☐☐☐☐

Valid from M M Y Y Expires M M Y Y

Security code* ☐☐☐ *Last 3 digits on the reverse of the card
ESSENTIAL IN ORDER TO PROCESS YOUR PAYMENT

Signature Date

We like to acknowledge all donations. However, if you do not wish to receive an acknowledgement, please tick here ☐

Please complete other side of form

Please return this form to:
BRF, 15 The Chambers, Vineyard, Abingdon OX14 3FE

BRF

The Bible Reading Fellowship is a Registered Charity (233280)

GUIDELINES SUBSCRIPTION RATES

Please note our new subscription rates, current until 30 April 2019:

Individual subscriptions
covering 3 issues for under 5 copies, payable in advance (including postage & packing):

	UK	Europe	Rest of world
Guidelines 1-year subscription	£16.95	£25.20	£29.10
Guidelines 3-year subscription (9 issues)	£46.35	N/A	N/A

Group subscriptions
covering 3 issues for 5 copies or more, sent to **one** UK address (post free):

Guidelines 1-year subscription	£13.50 per set of 3 issues p.a.

Please note that the annual billing period for group subscriptions runs from 1 May to 30 April.

Overseas group subscription rates
Available on request. Please email **enquiries@brf.org.uk**.

Copies may also be obtained from Christian bookshops:

Guidelines	£4.50 per copy

All our Bible reading notes can be ordered online by visiting **biblereadingnotes.org.uk/subscriptions**

For information about our other Bible reading notes, and apps for iPhone and iPod touch, visit **biblereadingnotes.org.uk**

GUIDELINES INDIVIDUAL SUBSCRIPTION FORM

All our Bible reading notes can be ordered online by visiting
biblereadingnotes.org.uk/subscriptions

☐ I would like to take out a subscription:

Title .... First name/initials .... Surname ....

Address ....

.... Postcode ....

Telephone .... Email ....

Please send *Guidelines* beginning with the September 2018 / January 2019 / May 2019 issue (*delete as appropriate*):

(*please tick box*)	UK	Europe	Rest of world
Guidelines 1-year subscription	☐ £16.95	☐ £25.20	☐ £29.10
Guidelines 3-year subscription	☐ £46.35	N/A	N/A

Total enclosed £ .... (cheques should be made payable to 'BRF')

Please charge my MasterCard / Visa ☐ Debit card ☐ with £ ....

Card no. ☐☐☐☐ ☐☐☐☐ ☐☐☐☐ ☐☐☐☐

Valid from ☐☐ ☐☐ Expires ☐☐ ☐☐ Security code* ☐☐☐

Last 3 digits on the reverse of the card

Signature* .... Date ....../....../......

*ESSENTIAL IN ORDER TO PROCESS YOUR PAYMENT

To set up a Direct Debit, please also complete the Direct Debit instruction on page 159 and return it to BRF with this form.

Please return this form with the appropriate payment to:
BRF, 15 The Chambers, Vineyard, Abingdon OX14 3FE

To read our terms and find out about cancelling your order, please visit **brfonline.org.uk/terms**.

The Bible Reading Fellowship is a Registered Charity (233280)

GUIDELINES GIFT SUBSCRIPTION FORM

☐ I would like to give a gift subscription (please provide both names and addresses):

Title .... First name/initials .... Surname ....

Address ....

.... Postcode ....

Telephone .... Email ....

Gift subscription name ....

Gift subscription address ....

.... Postcode ....

Gift message (20 words max. or include your own gift card):

....

....

Please send ***Guidelines*** beginning with the September 2018 / January 2019 / May 2019 issue (*delete as appropriate*):

(*please tick box*)	UK	Europe	Rest of world
Guidelines 1-year subscription	☐ £16.95	☐ £25.20	☐ £29.10
Guidelines 3-year subscription	☐ £46.35	N/A	N/A

Total enclosed £ .... (cheques should be made payable to 'BRF')

Please charge my MasterCard / Visa ☐ Debit card ☐ with £ ....

Card no. ☐☐☐☐ ☐☐☐☐ ☐☐☐☐ ☐☐☐☐

Valid from ☐☐ ☐☐ Expires ☐☐ ☐☐ Security code* ☐☐☐

Last 3 digits on the reverse of the card

Signature* .... Date ....../....../......

*ESSENTIAL IN ORDER TO PROCESS YOUR PAYMENT

To set up a Direct Debit, please also complete the Direct Debit instruction on page 159 and return it to BRF with this form.

Please return this form with the appropriate payment to:
BRF, 15 The Chambers, Vineyard, Abingdon OX14 3FE

BRF

To read our terms and find out about cancelling your order, please visit **brfonline.org.uk/terms**.

DIRECT DEBIT PAYMENT

You can pay for your annual subscription to our Bible reading notes using Direct Debit. You need only give your bank details once, and the payment is made automatically every year until you cancel it. If you would like to pay by Direct Debit, please use the form opposite, entering your BRF account number under 'Reference number'.

You are fully covered by the Direct Debit Guarantee:

The Direct Debit Guarantee

- This Guarantee is offered by all banks and building societies that accept instructions to pay Direct Debits.
- If there are any changes to the amount, date or frequency of your Direct Debit, The Bible Reading Fellowship will notify you 10 working days in advance of your account being debited or as otherwise agreed. If you request The Bible Reading Fellowship to collect a payment, confirmation of the amount and date will be given to you at the time of the request.
- If an error is made in the payment of your Direct Debit, by The Bible Reading Fellowship or your bank or building society, you are entitled to a full and immediate refund of the amount paid from your bank or building society.
- If you receive a refund you are not entitled to, you must pay it back when The Bible Reading Fellowship asks you to.
- You can cancel a Direct Debit at any time by simply contacting your bank or building society. Written confirmation may be required. Please also notify us.

The Bible Reading Fellowship

Instruction to your bank or building society to pay by Direct Debit

DIRECT Debit

Please fill in the whole form using a ballpoint pen and return it to:
BRF, 15 The Chambers, Vineyard, Abingdon OX14 3FE

Service User Number: | 5 | 5 | 8 | 2 | 2 | 9 |

Name and full postal address of your bank or building society

To: The Manager Bank/Building Society

Address

Postcode

Name(s) of account holder(s)

Branch sort code

Bank/Building Society account number

Reference number

Instruction to your Bank/Building Society

Please pay The Bible Reading Fellowship Direct Debits from the account detailed in this instruction, subject to the safeguards assured by the Direct Debit Guarantee. I understand that this instruction may remain with The Bible Reading Fellowship and, if so, details will be passed electronically to my bank/building society.

Signature(s)

Banks and Building Societies may not accept Direct Debit instructions for some types of account.